WORTHY TO RAISE ISSUES

WORTHY TO RAISE ISSUES

Preaching and Public Responsibility

James W. Crawford

The Pilgrim Press
Cleveland, Ohio

Acknowledgments

"Advent's Great Scandal" originally appeared in *Advent Christmas Sermons*, ed., Henry Rust. (Brea, Calif.: Educational Ministries, Inc., 1990) and is reprinted here with permission.

Scripture quotations are from the New Revised Standard Version Bible, copyright 1989, Division of Christian Education of the National Council of the Churches of Christ in the United States of America, and are used by permission.

Book design by Patricia Kellis. Cover design by Cindy Dolan.

Library of Congress Cataloging-in-Publication Data

Crawford, James W.
    Worthy to raise issues : preaching and public responsibility / James W. Crawford.
       p.   cm.
    Includes bibliographical references.
    ISBN 0-8298-0917-1 (alk. paper) :
      1. Congregational churches—Sermons. 2. Sermons, American. 3. Preaching. I. Title.
    BX7233.C78W67   1991
    252'.058—dc20   91-29272
                                        CIP

This book is printed on acid-free paper.

Printed in the United States of America.
10 9 8 7 6 5 4 3 2 1

The Pilgrim Press, Cleveland, Ohio

Contents

Preface

"The key problem is that today we do not have a profound public theology. That is we do not have a deep and broad concept of what God requires of humanity in our public behaviors in a broken, divided and threatened world." So writes Max Stackhouse in *Public Theology and Political Economy*, a plea for the churches to engage in the public arena with whatever influence they might muster intellectually, spiritually, politically. This book is one pastor's scattered attempt to articulate a public theology and to probe for the "deep and broad concepts" of those behaviors God requires of us "in a broken, divided and threatened world."

I have chosen the title *Worthy to Raise Issues* because that title describes members and friends of my congregation, the Old South Church in Boston, who throughout history have assumed that there is a tension between the implications of the gospel and the quality of life in society. The Introduction to the book outlines perceptual and theological tools I use to raise issues in our own time—one of these tools being the authority of the Old South Church's heritage. The Introduction also includes some ruminations on the risks of raising issues and the chance we may raise them "unworthily."

The main text consists of a body of sermons, most of them preached during the later years of the 1980s. These sermons touch on human perspectives and public policies those perspectives generate. The sermons attempt to bring biblical mandates and worldviews to bear on current public issues of political power, economic justice, and human community.

The world changes with astounding speed. Some specific issues come and go. No doubt some emphases the accompanying sermons reflect will have changed over the years. But the necessity of tackling issues remains. And though the particular components of an issue may change over time, in many cases the biblical perspective needed to understand the issue does not. For instance, the AIDS issue may change over the course of time. But the biblical mandates for public treatment of persons excluded by stigma bear hearing in every generation. The biblical mandates for inclusion are transferable from one specific public issue to another.

My hope in this book, then, is to offer fragments for a public theology. I trust they may provide substance and light for others.

Words of appreciation and acknowledgment, of course, know nearly no end:

- The congregation of the Old South Church in Boston, who year after year continue to offer encouragement and support, the time, and the livelihood necessary for study and preparation as well as family sustenance. I am a fortunate person to be serving amid such a generous people.

- The Church and Ministry Department of Andover Newton Theological School. Professors Meredith Handspicker, George Sinclair, Daniel Novotny, and their colleagues offered tremendous encouragement in helping me to think through the dimensions of this piece and how it might provide assistance to others in the ministry. This small volume began as a project in their doctoral program. I am grateful for their support.

- Professor Gabriel Fackre, teacher, advisor, confidant, friend. His careful reading of the manuscript and his availability for consultation and critique went far beyond the call of duty. His confidence lies behind this work. I will be forever grateful for his having written the Foreword to this volume.

- Barbara Withers of the Pilgrim Press. With no small amount of trepidation I walked into her New York office one day and asked if she would be good enough to read this book, make a judgment about its publishing possibilities, and then, if appropriate, edit it. She agreed. Her judgment, perception, and magnanimity have been a godsend.

- Henry Richardson Crawford, my eldest son, computer guru, late-night typist, and technical advisor who finally assembled, programmed, and printed the manuscript. He helped with tracking down sources. He made judgments on content. He served as proofreader extraordinaire. This book could never have been completed without his energy, wisdom, and ingenuity.

- Linda Lovett Crawford and our family, whose patience and understanding knew no end during those moments of anxiety and brooding in the course of sermon and book preparation. Words may indicate the truth of a matter, but in Linda's case they are truly inadequate.

James W. Crawford
Brookline, Massachusetts
Lent 1991

Foreword

In 1773 Samuel Adams led a band of colonists out the front door of the South Church Meetinghouse to dump British tea in Boston Harbor. The encounter with "the powers and principalities" has since continued at Old South—in ways usually less dramatic, and sometimes more. This important work by its present pastor gives us a glimpse of the preaching and action of a model that continues to be a living gospel witness in the world of public affairs.

In these pages the reader will learn from on-line preaching about both the theory and practice of mission to the city, and to the world beyond. We have here not a chronicle of achievements—though there are many of those, indeed—but a "public theology" that helped to make them possible. We find that doctrine is not a scholastic game or classroom exercise, but a framework for daily decisions about AIDS patients in a nearby hostel, the Dudley Street Neighborhood Initiative for the Homeless, Kip Tiernan's Poor People's Campaign, the furlough program for Massachusetts prisoners. . . . Old South puts its money and its bodies where its mouth is.

But the old Reformers were not ashamed of church talk too. They called the congregation a "mouth house." Deeds are impelled by words and need to be interpreted by intelligible tongues. Preaching is the crucial place where the mouth has its rightful say. So it has been for over three centuries at Old South, with its long line of prophetic voices.

The mouths of these preachers are not far from the eyes that both read books and write them. Pastor Crawford continues this tradition of learning. I know something about the scholarship behind the sermons found here, seeing Jim every Monday morning at Theological Tabletalk, our fifteen-year conversation among Boston pastors and teachers who weekly discuss weighty theological works. The hard-won intellectual struggles, the extensive exegetical labors that undergird proclamation and argument, may not always be obvious in the homilies that follow, but they are there. Indeed, the development of this book from doctoral studies at Andover Newton is yet another evidence of the intellectual rigor entailed in the preached Word.

Preaching in this work, and historically at Old South, clearly stands in the Reformed tradition, and does so in at least three respects. The first has to do with the firm belief in the Divine sovereignty that grounds all Old South social ministry. Nicholas Wolterstorff describes it as Calvinism's "world-formative" commitment. As with Calvin, who wanted Geneva to reflect something of the Divine glory, so with Crawford, who bears witness to the rule of God over the city of Boston.

In the second case, one finds it in the sobering judgment of our puny efforts to measure up to God's expectations, and thus an awareness of the fragility of human achievements. Time and again this preacher reminds us of the sin that persists in all our visionary ventures and the reality that buffets our dreams. The author brings his Niebuhrian realism to bear on the illusions of nineteenth-century utopianism, found in that period even in the world-formative pulpit of Old South.

The themes of both sovereignty and sobriety come together in the congregation's embrace of society's rejects. Old South is a house of hospitality for the vulnerable. Today that means solidarity with the homeless and the hapless. Yesterday it meant the misnamed "half-way covenant" of seventeenth-century Old South, in which a welcoming grace received the sinner and the pilgrim believer rejected by the exclusivism of a hyper-Puritanism. So in this church at the center of Boston is regularly heard the call to penitence and self-examination expressed by the author in Niebuhr's words:

> Our Gospel is one which assures salvation in the cross of Christ to those who heartily repent their sins . . . a revelation of the love of God only to those who first stand under its judgment.

The third refrain in the Reformed witness is the word of hope that resonates in all these sermons. A *sober* hope, yes, but for all that a dream that will not die. God has promised in this world portents of the great shalom to come. They are remarked here in the real, albeit ambiguous, fragments of liberation and reconciliation to be seen in the city and beyond. This hope is finally grounded in Easter faith, the resurrection theme that is heard so often by Old South parishioners. This theological indicative is inseparable from the public imperative, the joy that is partner to the cost. Indeed, the well-known Bonhoeffer linkage is regularly confessed in the United Church of Christ Statement of Faith used by the congregation:

> God calls us into the church to accept the cost and joy of discipleship.

As I sat in the Old South balcony on Easter Sunday recently, listening to Crawford preach about "hope in action" and looking around at the twelve hundred worshipers, I wondered about the media reports of a moribund mainline church. Yes, we fail and falter, Old South included. No, that is not the whole story. In the pages that follow, you will see some of the evidence of a grace too often unobserved. And that in an *old*-line as well as mainline congregation. May that grace abound, and this book be a "means of grace."

Gabriel Fackre

WORTHY TO RAISE ISSUES

Introduction

My bookshelf includes a volume entitled *The Public Vocation of Christian Ethics*.[1] The book includes reflection on "The Nuclear Age," "The Third World," "The Moral Assessment of Computer Technology," and the like. Although the articles are illuminating, it is the title itself that intrigues me. I believe Christian ethics has a public vocation. This public vocation of Christian ethics is born of the gospel itself. Saint John's conclusion that we love because God first loved us is crucial to the dynamic of the Christian life. It grounds Christian ethics. Any willingness of ours to face the risks inherent in making visible the realm of heaven in this world derives from gratitude we express for the reconciling, forgiving work God has done on our behalf through the events of the passion and resurrection of Jesus Christ. At the cross we see how "God treats other people"—namely, us. In the resurrection we see that treatment, for all the risk and resistance it may receive, vindicated. Our living of the Christian life, our pursuing "the public vocation of Christian ethics," emerges from our gratitude over Christ's way for others—indeed, for us.

This little volume, then, with its tilt toward the public vocation of Christian ethics, is an extended commentary on our grateful response to God's prior gift to us in Christ. It contains sermons preached over a number of years dealing theologically and biblically with public issues. I am convinced Christianity is not simply a matter of private disposition, a warm feeling in the heart, or a matter of "how I'm feeling today." Our faith surely touches our feelings, but finally, as Jesus suggests, the world will know us by our fruits (Matthew

1

7:20). And our fruits are borne not only in a private or domestic realm, they are borne as well in the public realm. The sermons in this collection were preached under the assumption that confessing Christians are public Christians, serving with energy, imagination, and love amid the broken public realm. They seek to equip the saints for a public ministry.

From where, then, one might ask, comes the title of this book, *Worthy to Raise Issues*? Upon entering the vestibule of the Old South Meetinghouse in downtown Boston, one sees a plaque reading:

> Here were the town meetings that ushered in the Revolution. Here Sam Adams, James Otis, and Joseph Warren exhorted. Here the men of Boston proved themselves independent, courageous, free men, worthy to raise issues which were to concern the liberty and happiness of millions yet unborn.

To be sure, those eighteenth-century meetings were not church meetings; they were town meetings. But they did take place in a church meetinghouse, and the populace gathered there wrestled with public issues of enormous contemporary import.

What follows here proceeds from the belief that church meetinghouses today harbor under their roofs men and women no less "worthy to raise issues." It proceeds convinced that with humility, insight, homework, courage, and not a little humor, public issues can be assessed and to some degree ameliorated by those who desire to encourage peace with justice in the human community. It proceeds convinced that biblical mandates can issue in public policy.

To live with such a conviction, of course, makes us vulnerable to many traps. Christians who have considered themselves "worthy to raise issues" down the centuries have frequently pursued those issues with such a sure sense of righteousness and purity as to engender vicious sectarian splintering and inhumane political cru-

sades. The results have evidenced themselves in op-
pressive theocratic oligarchy. Peace arrived, to be sure.
But it was the peace of oppression, uniformity, and
conformity.

So how do we raise issues today? What are the
perils and promises, the risks and possibilities, the
guidelines and lineaments for addressing "the public
vocation of Christian ethics"? For me, Reinhold Niebuhr
has served as a distant but ever-fresh mentor, and he
offers some clues. In one of his essays he asks the
question, "Can the church give a moral lead?"[2] After
reviewing a number of urgent current issues and refer-
ring to the no less urgent prodding of others to make
some moral judgment about those issues, Niebuhr writes:

> We must as Christians constantly make significant
> moral and political decisions amidst and upon per-
> plexing issues and hazardous ventures. We must
> even make them "with might" and not half heart-
> edly. But the Christian faith gives us no warrant to
> lift ourselves above the world's perplexities and to
> seek or to claim absolute validity for the stand we
> take. It does, however, encourage us to the charity
> which is born of humility and contrition. This is not
> a "clear moral lead" but a clear religious insight into
> the fragmentary character of all human morality,
> including the virtue of the saints and the political
> pronouncements of the churches. "Our life is his in
> Christ with God." If we claim to possess overtly what
> remains hidden we turn the mercy of Christ into an
> inhuman fanaticism.[3]

This book offers one pastor's concern to provide
some "moral fragments" reflecting on some of the troubling ethical dilemmas of our own time. It is one person's
attempt to raise issues.

The list of issues is, of course, partial. Each morning
we awaken to fresh headlines proclaiming public conflicts, conundrums, and choices demanding ethical judgments. The array of commentary surrounding these

issues is myriad. I am persuaded clergy are mandated to offer a perspective from the biblical tradition enabling church members to include this perspective as they decide what kind of world they really want and what they are willing to pay and to risk for it.

Conviction 1: The Biblical Faith Makes a Difference

There are, of course, a number of additional convictions lying behind these sermons. First of all, they are written from the deeply held belief that the biblical faith offers a perspective and commends a mode of conduct that can make a difference amid the trouble and possibility of our world. What is this perspective? What is it we have to say? Niebuhr offers another clue:

> Our Gospel is one which assures salvation in the cross of Christ to those who heartily repent of their sins. It is a gospel of the cross; and the cross is a revelation of the love of God only to those who have first stood under its judgment. It is in the cross that the exceeding sinfulness of human sin is fully revealed. It is in the cross that we become conscious how, not only what is worst, but what is best in human culture and civilization is involved in [human] rebellion against God.[4]

Niebuhr continues,

> Repentance is the first key into the door of the Kingdom of God. . . . Whenever [human beings] trust their own righteousness, their own achievements, whenever they interpret the meaning of life in terms of the truth in their own culture, or find in their own capacities a sufficient stepping stone to the holy and divine, they rest their life on a frail reed which inevitably breaks and leaves their life meaningless.[5]

Thus, a first conviction running through the accompanying sermons understands God's creation as one filled with possibilities for good, yet riddled with frailty and fragmented hopes, a world where the best of human beings ends up on a cross erected for the most civilized of reasons.

Conviction 2: Preaching from Hope

Secondly, these sermons are written from a deeply rooted hope. They arise from a conviction that the gospel proclaims hope against hope. Again, standing at the foot of the cross one sees starkly the "hopeless" nature of the human predicament. Tragedy strikes us at the cross of Christ. A question confronting the world and the Christian faith at the cross is always, "If life has meaning, if goodness makes a difference, if love has eternal dimensions, how could the best human being the world has known be crucified? If God is love, why did Jesus die?" The answer, of course, expresses the paradox of the gospel. The tragic event becomes itself the revelation of the lengths to which the God of love will go to hang on to the creation. Thus, when one asks the question, "Where was God when Jesus died?" faith's answer is, "God was there all the time." The identification of this God of Jesus Christ with the suffering of humankind and the power this God exercised, not in preventing or resisting the suffering, but working through it, assuring us of Divine solidarity with us even as we perceive abandonment—this is the backdrop against which the sermons are prepared.

Conviction 3: Centrality of Scripture

A third conviction sustaining these sermons emerges from my belief in the centrality of scripture to the integrity of our faith and life. The exegetical and expositional work evident in the sermons illustrates, I believe, a number of approaches to scripture.

Scriptural Approach A: Authority of Scripture

First, a note on the authority of scripture. These sermons are written out of faith in the God made vulnerable to the human condition. Just as God becomes human in Jesus, just as God allows Jesus to die, so the Bible is vulnerable to human contingency. The paradox of the God of Jesus Christ lies in our God's revelation through the most fragmentary, partial, and incoherent components of human life. God gives us no guarantees exclusive of our faith. The history of liberation we know through the biblical testimony comes to us filtered through hundreds of years of reflection, confused translations, lost manuscripts, sectarian propaganda, council compromises, conflicting positions. The Bible is a product of human frailty through which Almighty God reveals at once a majestic yet servant self. These human fragments testify to Someone beyond themselves. They are no less vulnerable to the flux, myopia, and intrigue of the human condition than the One who died on the cross. Yet, miracle of miracles, through these frail fragments we catch a glimpse of the liberating, servant God.

Scriptural Approach B: Scripture's Accessibility

A second approach to scripture assumes both the accessibility of the text to everyone as well as the excitement and challenge of rigorous textual study. I am, first of all, a true believer in the maxim "The Bible is every person's book." No scholar, preacher, professor, bishop, or pope can take from the hands, minds, and spirits of the faithful the rendering of the text. The Spirit continues to open new meaning and dimension to every reader with even the most exhausted of texts. Nonetheless, the community over time has also reflected on the text. With scholarly tools probing language, culture, metaphor, literature, history, and communication the biblical text takes on new facets, like a diamond shining from many different angles. So research, brooding, the search for contemporary illustrations, the efforts to craft a sentence expressing exactly what I want to transmit requires time with the Bible, books, scholarship, prayer—study.

Scriptural Approach C: Redaction Criticism

A third approach to scripture evident in these sermons reflects a tilt toward an exegetical stance we call "redaction criticism." This approach arises from the belief that early Christian communities existing some forty to sixty years after Jesus died faced issues seriously threatening their own faith, hope, and love. Persecution, contempt, and indifference from the world around them tended to erode the witness of some members of those primitive Christian communities. In addition, the inner life of the communities bordered on chaos. Some members made arrogant claims to special religious insight and authority. Others rejected outsiders who could not meet insiders' faith or behavior requirements. Still others threatened to tear apart the fabric of churches while arguing over trivia. The New Testament authors, living amid this debate and struggle, gathered up the fragments, the stories, the testimonies, the isolated traditions, reflections, and confessions treasured by their communities and applied them in coherent, creative, and redemptive fashion to their current troubles. They illuminated the meaning of Jesus Christ for their communities and the world through their own efforts to interpret and provide living witness to the gospel though surrounded by the terror, defeat, and apathy of their own time.

In much the same way, preachers today are redactors. We too, face external resistance and indifference to the gospel. We too, discover within our communities lukewarm faith, cynicism, and apathy. We too find ourselves arguing over minutiae having little to do with the treatment of other people. We too get confused over matters of communal and religious authority. The issues troubling our forebears in the early church trouble us no less. We can find clues to both the troubles and the gospel's approach to them by looking to the "redactors"—the most prominent among equals being Matthew, Mark, Luke, and John.

Conviction 4: Power and Its Stewardship

A fourth conviction running through these sermons reveals a wariness of power and its stewardship. This wariness has been articulated most profoundly for me, again, by Reinhold Niebuhr, in his defense of democracy, *The Children of Light and the Children of Darkness*. In his introduction, Niebuhr outlines the qualities of human nature encouraging and those imperiling democracy. They are, on the one hand, a pessimism about the possibilities of human factions' resolving their conflicting interests except through the wielding of a preponderant centralization of power. On the other hand, there may be such optimism about the capacities of human nature to resolve conflicting interests as to engender naïveté about the selfish interests at work, thus resulting in communal chaos. This too results in a civil yearning for unity, ending, probably, in tyranny. Niebuhr takes a middle path, recognizing both the optimistic aspects of human nature and the pessimistic. He writes:

> Man's capacity for justice makes democracy possible; but man's inclination to injustice makes democracy necessary. In all non-democratic political theories the state or the ruler is invested with uncontrolled power for the sake of achieving order and unity in the community. But the pessimism which prompts and justifies this policy is not consistent; for it is not applied, as it should be, to the ruler. If men are inclined to deal unjustly with their fellows, the possession of power aggravates this inclination. That

is why irresponsible and uncontrolled power is the greatest source of injustice.

The democratic techniques of a free society place checks upon the power of the ruler and administrator and thus prevent it from becoming vexatious. The perils of uncontrolled power are perennial reminders of the virtues of a democratic society; particularly if a society should become inclined to impatience with the dangers of freedom and should be tempted to choose the advantages of coerced unity at the price of freedom.

The consistent optimism of our liberal culture has prevented modern democratic societies both from gauging the perils of freedom accurately and from appreciating democracy fully as the only alternative to injustice and oppression. When this optimism is not qualified to accord with the real and complex facts of human nature and history, there is always a danger that sentimentality will give way to despair and that a too consistent optimism will alternate with a too consistent pessimism.[6]

One will find throughout the following sermons a similar understanding of human nature and the political realm.

Conviction 5: The Nature of Preaching

A fifth conviction undergirding the book's sermons rests on the nature of preaching. And here I wish to make five observations.

Observation A: Christ Saves Us in the World

First of all, I believe with David Buttrick that we interpret Jesus Christ in the light of our "being saved in the world."[7] The tone and emphasis of this work focuses on God's saving power transforming the life of human beings in this world. The sermons in the book reflect faith in the good intentions of God for human life. The book's sermons try to glimpse the possibilities of a new human community rooted and grounded in what Martin Luther King Jr. somewhere called the "forensic" love of God—an active, future-oriented, world-transforming power, ruling and transfiguring the nature of our existence.

Observation B: The Communal Context

Secondly, these sermons take seriously their communal context. They are written, of course, out of the convictions of the preacher, his experience, study, and concerns. But, at least as important, they are written for a particular congregation, meeting at a particular time, on a special corner in one of the world's great cities. I tend to believe preaching is cumulative—its impact on members of a congregation grows over time. To be sure, fifteen to twenty minutes on Sunday morning may be decisive for particular individuals. Preaching may be decisive on special occasions for a whole congregation. But preaching's most significant impact on a congregation registers after their becoming acquainted with the preacher, their hearing her emphasis, religious vocabulary, and hermeneutic week after week, year after year. Certain phrases, styles, understandings, and self-definitions begin to creep into the very marrow of the institution over time. Preaching is communal. It is cumulative.

Observation C: Preaching and Leadership

Thirdly, I believe preaching is closely tied to leadership. This is not to say other gifts of ministry such as pastoral care, teaching, or prophetic activity fail to enhance leadership. We all know congregations where preaching may not be the strong point of the leader. Surely his or her commitment and gifts in other areas provide ample authority to move the congregation toward the promised land. But I believe preaching and institutional leadership can go hand in hand. Preaching is not an isolated event. It motivates, inspires, recasts hopes, opens new horizons. A matrix of concern, conviction, and commitment to shared goals begins to take shape over a period of time. The preacher-leader and her congregation share a solidarity and mutual respect regarding ends, if not always means. In a congregation's decisions about participation in the public realm social goals may bring consensus while strategies and tactics trigger degrees of disagreement. Reaching the goals remains to be discussed, debated, and resolved. The processes for resolution require continuing articulation in formal and informal settings. They demand administration in the same settings. Preaching and leadership will occasionally pose troublesome dilemmas. But to recognize their symbiotic relationship lies at the very heart of my vocation.

Observation D: Time and Timelessness

A fourth observation about preaching, and indeed about the accompanying sermons, has to do with timeliness and timelessness. For the most part, the issues provoking the sermons in this book will be recognized as falling within a particular historical moment. They name names, places, and issues circumscribed by time. But one dares to assemble such material because the issues raised tend to reveal a particular gospel perspective that remains timeless. This, of course, is not unlike the Bible itself. We read about specific incidents with people and places. From them we discern truth about the ways of God with us. My hope is, time-bound though the accompanying sermons may be, they may transmit to the reader insight transcending the particular incidents that inspired them.

Observation E: Inclusiveness

One of the dramatic changes taking place over the lifetime of my ministry, and surely during the last decade in particular, involves inclusiveness. In the course of assembling this book I discovered a number of things this significant perceptual and political change has wrought.

First of all, of course, it demanded a thorough re-working of gender-exclusive language. As the pronouns for people and the metaphors for God we used were shown to be sexist and patriarchal, changes for the sake of justice and equality became imperative. Aesthetic considerations, historical accuracy, and previous assumptions needed to be altered for the gospel's sake. Except for the Bible quotations, you will not see the changes in the accompanying sermons, but be assured they were numerous. I stand grateful to the editor, Barbara Withers, for gently alerting me to a broad range of issues at stake.

Clearly this is a matter pressing directly on the work of any contemporary pastor, teacher, and preacher. A sermon in the accompanying collection, "Crowned with Glory and Honor," indicates why. The language we use bears with it the structure of the universe we live in. Male pronouns—for instance, "mankind" for the whole of the human family—does indicate that males may be the measure of humanity. Metaphors for God exclusively male carry an understanding of the very ground of creation where "men are in charge" and women take an inferior place. This, of course, is obvious to many. But many of us need to take pains in the preparation of our sermons and liturgies to sustain the full humanity of women and men in the economy of God.

A corollary to the above deals with the content of the notes and bibliography of this book. As this is written I happen to be in my mid-fifties, a Union Seminary graduate of 1962. As with many pastors and teachers, our theological libraries, sources, and language tend to reflect the years of our upbringing brought to crystallization by our seminary training. They were crucial in our spiritual and intellectual formation. Since my graduation from seminary, there has been an explosion of biblical and theological materials, particularly from the second and third worlds, from feminists, both men and women in the West, calling our attention to the limited perspectives of Eurocentric, Western, white males—such as the author of this book. This explosion demands our attention and, to a great degree, our spiritual appropriation. The content of symbols is being reperceived. Social analysis as bounced against the biblical faith has, at least currently, emerged from "below." Reality as perceived from the context of the disinherited and disfranchised, as against that perceived by the secure academicians and pastors of the middle classes, is increasingly a norm for our time. I suspect a compilation of sermons and essays dealing with public issues at the end of the century and assembled by a middle-aged, "mainline" preacher—regardless of the makeup of her congregation—will include in its bibliography a far broader range of biblical and theological resources than can be found in this one. The globalization of theological and biblical studies over this next decade will accelerate. No theologian–preacher–spiritual leader can afford to step aside from the rich and variegated resources washing down upon us.

Surely one of these new resources will consist of the New Revised Standard Version of the Bible. That translation is used throughout this book. It is clearly the first major standard translation making an attempt at significant inclusiveness. The NRSV's "people language" is inclusive of both genders. But "God language"? The masculine nouns and pronouns by and large remain. The translators protest that to change them would falsify the original patriarchal context and leave us with an inaccurate translation. Perhaps. But somehow this basic vehicle for the gospel we treasure must become increasingly reflective of the gospel's affirmation of our common humanity, male and female. I suspect the NRSV represents but the first salvo in an intense translation process dissolving the patriarchal world-view and making the Bible itself even more a sign of liberation.

Conviction 6: Social Ministry

Now, a sixth conviction underlying this book may be illustrated by what Dieter Hessel calls "social ministry."[8] Social ministry recognizes the institutional nature of a church, its being a community with financial resources, usually a building and property, members who vote and pay taxes—something more than just a loose association of individuals joining for some individualistic spiritual refreshment. The church is a body, larger than the sum of all its parts. In one way or another it is a community organization with dreams, expectations, and hopes about the nature of human community and destiny. As a body it may make an impact on bringing some of those dreams a little closer to fruition in its own community and across the world. Hessel describes the dilemma of every congregation as one seeming to divide congregants between the "rescuers" and the "transformers."[9] The rescuers are those who see others deeply affected by the distortions, injustices, and structural myopias of the larger polity. The rescuers seek to provide the "safety net" for those who fall through socioeconomic cracks. Rescuers support the shelters for the homeless, provide volunteers for the soup kitchens, contribute money for the tutoring programs, provide the kindnesses and the generosity that bear individuals through tough times. This is an absolutely vital ministry, and every church claiming the name of Christ ought to be involving its people in "rescuing."

But there is another ministry no less important. Hessel calls it the ministry of the "transformers."[10] It begins when the rescuers ask, "So why are people hungry? Why are there so many homeless? How come a majority or our prisoners are of one race? Why can't the kids read?" The answers to these questions are not clear-cut. Indeed the underlying issues are myriad.

Poverty, race, overcrowding, gender discrimination, power abuse, corporate greed, political self-interest, the lack of health and other social insurance, job dislocations—all of these and more create social pathologies engulfing whole communities. The transformers are those who seek to alleviate social problems by dealing with causes. Every church needs both rescuers and transformers! But to some degree the church as a body can function as a transformer. It bears corporate influence. It speaks for a constituency. It can bring to bear the high calling of the gospel upon inertia-bound, interest-riddled political and economic structures. The transformers are eager to change the status quo generating the problems in which the rescuers find themselves so deeply immersed. Individuals and churches can serve as both rescuers and transformers. Yet churches tend to find themselves involved predominantly in rescuing. These accompanying sermons take rescuing seriously. They also believe the church can be a transforming force, a component among social institutions leveraging change in unjust status quos.

Conviction 7: Public Theology

A seventh conviction underlying the book's sermons lays stress on the necessity and possibility of a "public theology." Heaven knows times have changed, so that a voice from one tradition is simply an element of the cacophony in this pluralistic world. A century ago the prophetic voices and institutions within so-called "mainline Protestant Christianity" would make the front pages of the urban dailies on Monday morning. Not so any more. Indeed, the cacophony has become so raucous and fragmented that, as Richard Neuhaus suggests, as far as theology dealing with civil and public morale is concerned, we live amid a "naked public square."[11] Neuhaus may be correct in his assessment. And I agree with Max Stackhouse when he writes,

The key problem is that today we do not have a profound public theology. That is, we do not have a deep and broad concept of what God requires of humanity in our public behaviors in a broken, divided and threatened world. To be sure, we have all sorts of voices speaking out of petty little contexts and attempting to tell us that this or that "biblical politics" is the absolute revelation. And we have "civil religions" of a number of stripes all over the globe. Class and ethnic ideologies wearing the garb of religion also abound. Not infrequently, these become powerful and begin to affect national or international policies. But what we do not have is a reliable "science" by which we could assess the relative sense or nonsense of such postures. Indeed, we do not have a common language for speaking of theological matters in the public domain, of what the ultimate reality behind human life in community entails. The language of public moral and spiritual discourse is fractured. People place their technical or economic or political bets on what will bring advantage without paying conscious attention to the governing principles and purposes of life.[12]

I make no claim that the sermons in this book are any more than fractured pieces making their way into the public domain and discourse. They are an attempt, however, to be a sample of what Stackhouse calls for when he invites the ecumenically oriented churches to reclaim "their greatest treasure": "a capacious theology, defensible in public discourse, that is able to link personal and social matters, ideal and material reality, memory and hope, private and public vision."[13]

Conviction 8: The Authority of the Old South Church

And, lastly, a conviction underlying the presenting of these sermons rests on the history of the Old South Church itself. Earlier we mentioned the high calling of

church members, "worthy to raise issues." The history of
the Old South provides ample authority for raising issues, for wrestling with the public vocation of Christian
ethics. In guidebooks and other Boston memorabilia the
Old South is described as "historic." Why? Because
throughout its 320 years the congregation has taken
initiatives making an impact on both public and ecclesial
life. It reflects a history of public and theological activ-
ism. It has traditionally embodied a sensitivity to the
times. Let me offer just a sampling of its public impact.

The church was founded in 1669 by second- and
third-generation Bostonians. They founded the church
under severe duress. The first generation of Puritans
were so sure of their piety and doctrine they tended to
view their children and their children's children as spiritually inadequate. The founders of our Puritan churches
measured their progeny's spiritual experience against
their own and found their children's spirituality want-
ing. The founders' requirement for baptism and church
membership: conversion must be approved by one's forebears. All too often, the forebears disapproved. As a
result of negative judgments on their Christian piety
and experience, a vast number of potential church members from the second and third generations were refused
membership. The churches began to die for lack of
members. What to do? A rump delegation from the First
Church of Boston gathered a new congregation committed to loosening requirements for both baptism and
church membership. The old orthodoxies began to
crumble. The established congregations put up enormous resistance to this upstart, heretical congregation.
The General Court was petitioned to stamp it out. Synod
agendas included debates to kill it. Theocrats sought
to subvert it. Nevertheless, in the face of this tremendous resistance, a new congregation, a "liberal" congregation, the Third Church in Boston, taking on
both church and state, uneasy with the status quo,
was founded.

A second significant encounter in the public realm took place during the period of the American Revolution. The former historian of the commonwealth, Richard Hale, once remarked in casual conversation, "The American Revolution was a struggle between the deacons of the Old South Church and the king's Parliament." And so it was. William Dawes, a deacon of the church, rode with Paul Revere and Samuel Prescott to warn the militias in Lexington and Concord of the pending British incursion on April 18, 1775. The Old South has always laid claim to Benjamin Franklin, baptized in icy water in January 1706, described by Justice Holmes as a "citizen of Boston who lived for a while in Philadelphia," and later accused by his British antagonists as being "the most dangerous man in America." Samuel Adams, the fiery propagandist of revolution, served as a deacon of the Old South. The "Boston Tea Party," that shocking and mutinous event contemptuously throwing off royal authority, began as a political rally in the Old South Meetinghouse. The church and its membership took public responsibility.

In the course of the nineteenth century, many theological commitments with public implications emerged. The Old South Church, its ministers and members, helped found the City Mission Society. During the Civil War the congregation was often split over the question of abolition. The minister, Jacob Manning, courageously spoke for justice and served as chaplain of a Massachusetts regiment.

In 1875 the congregation moved into its new Back Bay meetinghouse. That move came after an intense public discussion about the meetinghouse as a patriotic shrine. How could the congregation leave its ancestral home with all its memories and glorious associations? The prayer offered by Jacob Manning at the dedication of the new building set its purpose in proper context:

> Take this building, O Thou Great Head of the Church, to whom we now bring it. Make it Thy own temple

and make us Thy living temples. Use it for the glory of Thy holy kingdom, and keep us the loyal subjects of that kingdom. Spare it only so long as it shall serve Thy loving purpose, and spare and bless us only that we may declare Thy name. When its noble walls must crumble, teach Thy people to bow in the faith of something better to come; and when our spirits must be unclothed of their earthly house, may they rise to be clothed upon with the house which is in heaven.[14]

In 1884 the congregation elected George Gordon as pastor of the church. Surrounding this ministry there emerged the great theological controversies of the late nineteenth century. I have often thought George Gordon fought the so-called "modernist" controversies some four decades before Harry Emerson Fosdick faced the wrath of the Presbyterians in the 1920s. Gordon sought to recast the outlook and attitude of New England Congregationalism. His efforts triggered resistance. At his installation Gordon met intellectual hostility as well as the refusal of colleagues to vote for the affirmation of his "call." Some participants walked out of the meeting. One of the "dropouts" refused to participate in the installation service.

How shall we categorize this important religious figure, George A. Gordon? He comes to us somehow as a mixed blessing. On the one hand he sought to make sense of the Christian tradition to his contemporaries. He touched many of the major issues of his own time and tried to pursue the public vocation of Christian ethics. He surely caught the spirit of his age.

And what was that spirit? A sense of constant experimentation, perennial evolution to higher forms, industrialization, the triumph of technique over the problems besetting humankind, the possibility of the Christian faith's carrying the world, an optimism about the future—all this represented the mood of the time. Again, orthodoxies came under fire. In a sermon entitled "The

Eternal Pledge of Progress," George Gordon joined the spirit of the age to the attributes of the Divine.

> Progress is by divine authority; it is by divine decree; it is by divine necessity. So long as God's purpose in Christ remains unovertaken, the new insight and the new love must register an advance upon the old. It has pleased God to move his goal through development; it has pleased him thus to perfect his work. It is the ever mightier coming of the Holy Spirit in the mind of the church that renders the past obsolete. Again, it must be said that God is the great innovator; it is he that discredits the thoughts of men about his kingdom; it is he that supersedes the old by the new.[15]

Yet, as much as anyone, Gordon illustrates the risks of our being overwhelmed by the "spirit of the age." Even as he attempted to articulate a theological stance that could be grasped by the men and women of his own time, even as he stood against doctrinaire and rigorous Calvinist scholastics, Gordon allowed the "eternal pledge of progress" to veil the tragic element in the human condition. As Reinhold Niebuhr indicates, Gordon represented a generation inventing and selling "schemes of redemption from evil which made repentance unnecessary."[16] Gordon, for all of his creativity and his courageous break with a stifling orthodoxy, spoke for the "liberal part of our culture," tending to believe that "the Christian idea of the sinfulness of all men was outmoded."

> In its place it put the idea of a harmless egotism, rendered innocuous either by prudent self-interest or by a balance of all social forces which would transmute the selfishness into a higher social harmony. The vanity of that idea was proved by the ever more dynamic disproportions of power in our society and the ever greater destruction of community in a technical society. Sometimes the liberal part of our cul-

ture conceived the idea of redemption through growth and development ("the eternal pledge of progress!"). Men suffered (so it was argued) not from sin but from impotence. But fortunately the whole historical process was itself redemptive. It translated man from impotence to power, from ignorance to intelligence, from being the victim to becoming the master of historical destiny. This illusion proved as tragic as the first one. Since the sin of man lies in the corruption of his will and not in his weakness, the possibilities of evil grow with the development of the very freedom and power which were supposed to emancipate man.[17]

Simply speaking, the grand progressive perspectives of the late nineteenth century collapsed in the carnage of World War I, the Great Depression, and the bloody twentieth century. Gordon's monumental efforts "to read the signs of the times" and to be in tune with the "spirit of the age," eloquent and inspiring though they may have been for those riding the crest of nineteenth-century technical power and knowledge (and the Old South Church was filled with them)—Gordon's effort fell short because he tended to remove the cross from its inevitability in our pursuing the reign of God and its centrality to our ultimate redemption. Those eager to make our gospel "relevant" need be wary of the same risk.

The last six decades at Old South might be called the "urban church years." The Social Gospel made a distinct impact on the life of the church. What had been primarily a great preaching station began to broaden its self-understanding and missionary vocation. The church erected a parish house in 1932. It included a massive kitchen, dining hall, function rooms, and drama stage. Downtown churches began to pick up neighborhood responsibilities. The YMCA and the downtown church began to overlap activities. Social services in church buildings became the order of the day. The church became a social center, a service agency.

A sign and symbol of this change could be seen in
the Old South's pastor, Russell Henry Stafford (minister from 1927 to 1945). Following George Gordon was
no easy task, and during Stafford's first two years at
Old South, Gordon continued to be present in the chan-
cel. But Stafford, although a fine scholar-preacher himself, was impatient with Old South's limiting itself to
Sunday morning worship. Although the Depression affected Old South no less than other major institutions,
the church made the effort to recast itself into more of
an agency for local social service and action. Indeed,
as the world anticipated war in 1940, the director of
social services at the church began his annual report
with the words,

> To all Christians today the world either looks hope-
> less or presents a very real challenge for service. . . .
> The fact is that in recent years material progress has
> outdistanced social gains. It is for us to discover in
> what new and unexplored regions the old spirit of
> service must become a pioneer in order to close this
> chasm and keep civilization moving forward."[18]

And Dr. Stafford himself set a tone recognizing the
place of the gospel in a changing world, the war-threat-
ened world of 1940. Recognizing that troubled times
call out the deepest resources of the gospel, Stafford
invited parishioners to recommit themselves to the
"Kingdom of God." His words are noble for his and any
other time:

> We need to feel and know that in a situation well
> nigh impossible from every secular point of view,
> political, economic and military, with destruction ram-
> pant and raging everywhere, we are nevertheless in
> a position to do something, however little, that shall
> count constructively toward peace among men and
> the coming of God's Kingdom. . . . In the long run,
> nothing but [the influence of Jesus] can ever last-
> ingly quell human savagery and bring a general

transformation of the general mind and heart from hatred to love as its dominant one. And to sow the seed of that influence by word and deed, though it fall for a moment out of sight and seem to die, is to make provision for a harvest of righteousness that shall yet ripen under the sun. . . . So long as we go on supporting the Gospel by gift and prayer in all the earth, we may be sure that under the inevitable surface wreckage of war we are still helping to lay the firm foundation of a new and better world order.[19]

In the years following World War II, the church went from strength to strength. It flowered with the great religious renaissance during the fifties and early sixties. Its minister, Frederick M. Meek, was a superb leader. His mind and heart brooded always on the significance of the gospel and the ministry of the church for the life of the city and the world. Through the postwar era, the days of Senator McCarthy, the Korean War, the tremendous population upheavals of the sixties and seventies, and the Vietnam War, Frederick Meek alerted the congregation to the great questions posed by the gospel to the transient issues of the times. Reminiscing in 1966, after twenty years at Old South, using the religious language of his time, Dr. Meek offered what would be the touchstone of all his twenty-seven years at Old South. In perplexing and rapidly changing times, the basic question, he insisted, is always:

"How does this or that affect the worth, the dignity, the value of man, of people, as God the Father Creator has purposed it?" Before that question, the use of science's complicated and awesome discoveries, the planning of the bureaucrats, the bills that Congress and the State House vote, the civic planning of our city, the uncertainties that beset us in war's violence and in the races' relations, the vexing questions of morality, the chosen direction of our lives and our day by day deeds are all to be examined. Making this fact known is the primary mission of the Church. If you have never believed actually in the mission of the Church you had better believe in it now.[20]

And today, the Old South exists amid a shifting, churning, urban setting. If one can excuse some regional chauvinism, it can be said that Copley Square, Boston, Massachusetts, is one of the great urban crossroads of North America. Boston is in some ways an overgrown New England town, compact geographically on the one hand, yet hardly immune to the serious social pathologies of the late twentieth century on the other. The church includes among its congregants a wide variety of urban citizenry, yet it consists of a narrow slice of both urban culture and religious tradition. The church's location, however, and its high calling to be a servant, the invitation chiseled into the Roxbury pudding stone over the portico on Boylston Street—"Behold I Set Before You an Open Door"—draw into it hundreds of people representing the modern city. The larger public makes a claim on the church's resources, staff, and space no less than the "membership." Like hundreds of other downtown churches in North America, we seek to touch many bases, serve many needs, and tackle many problems. Our successes are limited, our ministry in many of its dimensions mediocre and inadequate. But, for all our own limitations, cultural constraints, and religious myopia, we live within a conviction that, in Reinhold Niebuhr's words:

> the Christian Gospel which transcends all particular and contemporary social situations can be preached with power only by a church which bears its share of the burdens of immediate situations in which men are involved, burdens of establishing peace, of achieving justice and of perfecting justice in the spirit of love. Thus is the Kingdom of God which is not of this world made relevant to every problem of the world.[21]

Thus this book. It stands in a long tradition of Old South Church life. It offers another illustration of the church's effort to wrestle with public issues theologically. It uses the language of our day to come to terms with the issues of our day. It includes samples of one church's efforts to make a difference in the quality of life in God's world. It is but a snapshot. Life will continue to change, time will make "ancient good uncouth," and in years hence men and women of the churches in Boston—and I trust in the Old South Church—will remain "worthy to raise issues which concern . . . the liberty and happiness of millions yet unborn."

PART ONE

Human Community

1 Can We Be Faithful Despite Worldly Opposition?

Introduction

What does it mean to be faithful in late twentieth-century America? Where lie those elements tempting, inviting, or even bludgeoning us into infidelity to our mission? The answer, of course, lies in a number of places. It certainly lies within and among ourselves. The New Testament is very clear about the hypocrisy, the faithlessness, the cynicism, and the overweening self-interest of Christians and their churches. We can be our own worst enemy.

But in some cases there is, indeed, another antagonist. And it can come from the "powers that be." These antagonists are not always ecclesiastical or religious powers; they may be secular and political powers as well. Among the most dangerous of antagonists are those who clothe their selfish objectives, power grabs, and privileged status in pious language. Religious people do this all the time. But so do the so-called "secular powers." In the name of some lofty or divine mandate they crush, manipulate, and destroy. We see such self-deception in nation-states and politicians identifying their own ends with some divine destiny. Indeed, the national identity of the United States is immersed in mythology grounded in biblical metaphors. Resistance to truly prophetic religion often comes from political structures wedded to the status quo and surrounding themselves with quasi-divine trappings.

This sermon, delivered in Lent, 1989, tackles the age-old issue of faithful men and women, their religious associations, and how these can lead to complacency or responsibility, blindness to public needs or courage to take on our necessary public tasks.

Can you live the Christian life? Can I? Can this beloved church of ours? We ask this question during Lent because the passages read in churches around the world during these seven weeks put the question starkly:

29

What does it mean to be a Christian in this world? Does it entail a certain kind of doctrinal stance? Should we appropriate a particular pious lingo to differentiate ourselves? Is it the way we sing hymns, order our worship, say our prayers? What does it mean to be Christian?

Luke offers us a clue. And the offer comes suggesting little of what we usually deem to be religious practice. There are no so-called spiritual disciplines here, as important as they may be. Luke shows Jesus being warned by some sympathetic friends against Herod's murderous designs. "Get out of here and hide!" they admonish him. "Herod has dispatched his death squads. Your assassination guarantees keeping the peace." Do you recall Jesus' response? Does he plan an escape? Hardly. "Tell that two-faced, conniving Herod, Jerusalem remains my objective!" Jesus exclaims. "I will confront that troubled city with a new way of life. And no doubt the city will treat me with the same contempt, rejection, and silencing it has inflicted on all those who sought to transform it."

What does Jesus show us here? Courage, patience, resolution, a relentless commitment to carry his mission to dangerous precincts, a dark foreboding that what he does carries with it terrible risk and danger. In looking at Jesus we see that living the Christian life means confronting the world with a way of organizing itself that shakes up the current order. Jesus shatters privilege, disperses power, crumbles elites, dissolves hierarchies, subverts credentials, redefines success. Why else would priests and kings want Jesus out of the way? We need to be clear: the trip Jesus takes to Jerusalem is not a simple religious pilgrimage. And what happens to him there is no ethereal, sentimental occasion of a pathetic innocent getting himself killed by mistake. Jesus' death is no mistake. A bunch of respectable, legitimate leaders and institutions want him out of the way. Religious, political, and military leadership conspire to wipe him out. They provoke his death. They premeditate violence. The generals, the judges, the ministers, the bishops, the priests, the magistrates, and the mob find themselves so badly threatened by this back-country visionary and liberator that they band together—many of them until that moment were mutual enemies—to protect and sustain the status quo. Herod, for instance: Caesar mandates Herod to keep the peace in that imperial backwater. Herod already faces wild insurrections and apocalyptic crazies in- tent on destroying Roman rule in the province. If this Jesus is another one of those revolutionary fanatics, Herod will liquidate him.

And the Pharisees, the religious establishment? They see an upstart with no credentials, no schooling, a Galilean outsider who has spent most of his life rubbing shoulders with "pagans." Jesus claims religious authority, but he breaks moral rules. He ignores religious convention. What can the Pharisees do? You can hear them now: "Silence the atheist before he poisons our membership, subverts our authority, and leaves us looking like frauds." And the military? They just obey orders.

No, when Jesus shrugs off the friendly advice of those renegade Pharisees who suggest he take to the hills, he well knows a miserable and bloody crisis will shortly occur. He knows those who wreak violence to sustain their status, privilege, and the public order will not hesitate to remove him forcibly, too.

Is there much difference between Jesus' time and our own? Surely in some situations we see the same terrible social crises. In Chile just recently, the army moved against the archbishop because he defended human rights. We look at South Africa. An apartheid regime, in the name of law and order and undergirded by religious rationale, engages in jailing, silencing, torturing, and exiling those who advocate and seek to inaugurate a multiracial, democratic, and just society.

But what about right here? What goes on in the good old U.S.A.? What about our nation, our politicians, our church leaders, our church people? What kind of courage, resolution, patience, purpose, and commitment do we demonstrate as we encounter the Herods and Pharisees of our world and time? Is crucifixion just around the corner for you, for me, for this church?

Not likely. In this country we Christian types are, by and large, patsies. We tip our hats to Herod. We accommodate ourselves to the mood and tone of the times. We are just like anybody else. We want discipleship. But that trip to Jerusalem—thanks, but no thanks!

Look, for instance, at President Bush's inauguration. I can hear some of you saying right now, "Hey, Jim, hold it a second! The honeymoon's not over." And I reply, "As a citizen, I agree. But as a church person, that's just my point." How did the inauguration start? Did you see a religious personage on the West Porch of the Capitol, risking his life to be there? Hardly. Billy Graham delivered the invocation. Now, I thank heaven for Billy Graham. He is a man of enormous personal integrity and profound faith. But to some degree he illustrates, it seems to me, the risks of a Christianity that cozies up to power rather than speaking truth to power.

I shall never forget one of the great sermons of the last twenty-five years, preached at the Riverside Church by Ernest T. Campbell, entitled "An Open Letter to Billy Graham." In that sermon, Dr. Campbell composed a searing plea to Graham on the occasion of the saturation bombings of North Vietnam on Christmas Eve, 1972. Richard Nixon had just been elected to his second term. Billy Graham was one of President Nixon's close friends and, in many ways, his personal pastor. That is perfectly fine. But the President had just announced "Peace is at hand," and here were massive bombings designed to drive the Vietnamese to their knees, killing thousands of others in the name of peace. Dr. Campbell suggested to Billy Graham:

> As one of the near voices within hearing distance of the throne, you surely bear a responsibility to critique government policy as well as to bless it. The president needs a Micaiah, not a Zedekiah; a prophet, not a mere house chaplain.[1]

Now, friends, what Ernest Campbell said in 1972 holds for 1989. As much as we Christians may love to hear Billy Graham pray for the President and our country; as much as we delight in the President's attending church regularly—indeed, even hours before his inauguration—our President and our country desperately need from Christians "a Micaiah, not a Zedekiah; a prophet, not a mere house chaplain."

So long as millions go homeless in our land;
so long as tens of thousands of kids find they are headed for nowhere but booze and drugs and jail;
so long as hundreds of billions of dollars are poured into armaments, security, and defense;
so long as national security becomes the slogan masking illegal, unethical, arbitrary acts of national policy;
so long as children starve while there's enough food to feed the world;
so long as gays and lesbians struggle against social, political, and economic stigmas;
so long as excellent health care goes primarily to the privileged;
so long as we buy that shrewd phrase "We've got the will but not the wallet," when, indeed, the truth lies 180 degrees in the other direction: we've got the wallet but not the will";
so long as any of this remains on the public agenda,

the man or woman presiding over the system where such poverty, injustice, and distorted priorities exist

has no need of a court priest or a house chaplain.
Rather, she has need—he has need—of discerning, relentless, patient, persevering biblical prophets. What
Dr. Campbell said to Billy Graham holds for all of us in
the churches, in this and every time:

> You have a unique opportunity to give dramatic
> definition to a form of evangelism that is equally
> comfortable confronting men and women with the
> claims of the Gospel, or calling the nation to a new
> fidelity to social righteousness. Migrant workers,
> welfare families, prisoners, ghetto school children,
> American Indians and many others would be heart-
> ened by your advocacy. Given the kind of world we
> have today, withheld advocacy on the part of Chris-
> tians gives substance to the charge that our faith
> is irrelevant.
>
> The Gospel needs to be articulated in our society;
> but it can also be argued that the Gospel needs very
> much to become incarnate in our society, in the form
> of persons who are willing to use their power on
> behalf of the powerless. The Word made flesh should
> not be made mere word again.[2]

House chaplain? Relentless prophet? We Christians
need to be wary of an eagerness for discipleship without
a will to take on the risks of Jerusalem.

Dare we continue Christ's ministry? What does it
take? It takes a gut refusal to accept as final the
structures of this world. It takes a refusal to accept,
finally, the world's presidents and congresses, its financial institutions and religious dogmas, its nationalism,
creedalism, gender discrimination, and ethnic obsessions, its denominationalism, security paranoia—an ada-
mant refusal to accept as final the very things forging
the cross of Jesus.

We are called to set ourselves against those forces
crucifying Jesus. We are called to live as if the cross is
not inevitable. We know this is a world where the likes

of Jesus and his commitments will always raise the resistance and mockery, the cynicism and contempt, of those who claim privilege and status by virtue of genes, money, or office. We know Jesus set out for Jerusalem, that his kind of life is frequently snuffed out, and that what happened to him in his quest for God's new world can happen to us. But that is the kind of world we are called to change. We are to be seeking, searching, working for a world where no one deems it necessary to inflict crucifixion on anyone else to save his own skin.

I conclude with the words of one who just this week took the risks of the Jerusalem journey. Allan Boesak, a minister of the Dutch Reformed Mission Church in South Africa, joined some one hundred hunger strikers rallying against a regime that was detaining them without charge, holding them incommunicado, denying basic human rights. Boesak—himself a victim of the regime's jailing, silencing, and house arrest—offers us, it seems to me, a place to stand as we seek to be faithful Christians in our own troubled and tumultuous times. Speaking to the World Council of Churches in 1983, Boesak said:

> The truth that the Messiah reveals is contrary to the lies, the propaganda, the idolatry, the untrustworthiness in the world. His truth is the truth that holds the freedom and the life of the world. And this we are called to proclaim. And so . . . let us affirm his truth and let us believe:
>
> — It is not true that this world and its inhabitants are doomed to die and be lost —
> *This* is true: For God so loved the world that he gave his only begotten son, that whosoever believes in him shall not perish but have eternal life.
> — It is not true that we must accept inhumanity, discrimination, hunger, poverty, death and destruction —
> *This* is true: I have come that they may have life, and have it abundantly.

- It is not true that violence and hatred shall have the last word, and that war and destruction have come to stay forever —
This is true: For unto us a child is born, unto us a Son is given, and the government shall be upon his shoulder, and his name shall be called wonderful counsellor, mighty God, everlasting Father, Prince of peace.
- It is not true that we are simply victims of the powers of evil that seek to rule the world —
This is true: To me is given all authority in heaven and earth, and lo I am with you, even unto the end of the world.
- It is not true that we have to wait for those who are specially gifted, who are the prophets of the Church, before we can do anything—
This is true: I will pour out my Spirit on all flesh, and your sons and your daughters shall prophesy, your young men shall see visions, and your old men shall have dreams. . . .
- It is not true that our dreams for the liberation of humankind, of justice, of human dignity, of peace are not meant for this earth and for this history —
This is true: The hour comes, and it is now, that the true worshippers shall worship the Father in spirit and in truth. . . .

So let us dream, let us prophesy; let us see visions of love, and peace and justice. Let us affirm with humility, with joy, with faith, with courage: *Jesus Christ— the Life of the World.*[3]

From "Jesus Christ, the Life of the World" in *If This is Treason, I Am Guilty* by Allan A. Boesak, copyright 1987 by Wm. B. Eerdmans Publishing Co., Grand Rapids, Michigan. Used by permission.

2 God's Love Endures Forever

Psalm 136 and Mark 16:1-8

Introduction

Easter, of course, represents the apotheosis of Christian faith, hope, and love. In churches everywhere vast crowds anticipate the metaphors and symbols of hope mediated by the sermon, the music, the prayers, the aesthetic adornments and decoration attendant upon the Easter liturgy. The roots of the Easter message lie in God's raising Jesus from the dead. It is about power. Easter signifies the power, to be sure, that re-creates beyond death, as Paul indicates, a "spiritual body" with all the implications for the integrity, goodness, and mystery of human life that entails. But, in addition, Easter proclaims power capable of overcoming and transforming the deadly propensities of the human condition resulting in our abuse, cruelty, injustice, and carelessness to and of one another.

This latter emphasis is one most Easter church attendees seldom anticipate. They come with a vague expectation the Easter sermon will deal primarily with matters of life after the grave, that the New Testament reference to "eternal life" promises something continuing for themselves, their family, their friends. They perceive of Easter as a glorified funeral service. This is partly on, but mostly off, the mark. Easter services and Easter preaching provide an opportunity to focus on God's promised victory over all those things getting us down, doing us in, and figuratively, as well as literally, killing us. Easter liturgies and preaching can convey hope for the restoration of relationships grown cold. They can proclaim hope for God's intended human community to live in peace rooted in justice. They can affirm the power exercised by a God of love to finally save us for life from all the manifestations of death, including our biological termination. They can offer an affirmation of a God sovereign over everything making an impact on human life and destiny.

The psalmist looks back over a long history. What does the psalmist see? Oppression under the heel of one of the earth's malevolent empires. The psalmist remembers a vast freedom movement rending the empire, liberating his people, defeating the forces of oppression. This poet sees slaves become free and recalls the hand of God moving, through sometimes utter hopelessness, saving, releasing. What can one say in celebration of liberation? How can one offer thanksgiving after perhaps five hundred years of blood and struggle, failure and survival? "O give thanks," our psalmist sings, recounting the story:

> Give thanks to this God of gods, who rules the universe, the sun, the moon, the stars. Give thanks to this Eternal One, this Sovereign of all royalty, who rules history. In our struggle for liberation, for freedom, for peoplehood, against all odds, we know God's love endures forever.
>
> —Psalm 136 (paraphrase)

This morning we claim the psalmist's story too—and the psalmist's faith. Yet on Easter Day we celebrate another saving event. It too proclaims freedom, liberation, salvation against rugged odds. It too emerges from our human story, a story really brought to focus by the last week of Jesus' life. Do you remember that last week? Talk about rugged odds. Nothing went right! The week began with a grand procession on Sunday. It ended in disaster on Friday. Those six days festered with confrontation and betrayal, fear and contempt, expediency and cynicism, and, finally, execution.

What happened on Sunday morning? We do not know. The four Gospels themselves do not agree. Those who search for evidence ask, "Did the women show up at the wrong tomb?" They ask if perhaps, unbeknown to the disciples, someone had snatched the body. Or they wonder if the disciples removed the body and invented the story. They question Easter as one grand hallucination. They ask if Jesus somehow survived the ordeal, walked out of the tomb, and died in bed. Somehow that search for the evidence intrigues us. But finally it fails. The Gospels are not biography. They are not investigative reporting. The authors wrote them from the absolute conviction that, through everything, God's love endures forever. They affirm *that*, first of all. And how should they talk about it but by lapsing into language of flesh and blood, gardens and tombs, angels and Sunday suppers turned from despair into joy?

At the heart of each story, however, stand the women. In Mark, it is Mary Magdalene, Mary the mother of James, and Salome. They go to care for Jesus' body and discover it gone. Someone on the scene cushions their alarm and sends them to Peter with the news. What a vivid picture! The news transforming the disciples, establishing the church, shattering the world, setting bells to ringing and trumpets to bursting is given, one shadowy morning, to a skittish trio of women, stumbling among some tombs in search of a corpse. I note from time to time, though less frequently these days than in the past, that an argument against women in the ministry—or the priesthood—hinges on Jesus' having chosen twelve men to proclaim the secrets of God's realm. Where were those twelve men, pray tell— any of them—on that Sunday morning when the news of a world changed forever was entrusted to women? I will tell you where. One of them was out committing suicide. Eleven were in hiding. And when the women announced their discovery, the men brushed it off as a bad joke. Jesus himself, confronting this pathetic fraternity, censured them for their incredulity and stupidity. So much for male pretensions to exclusive possession of the "keys of the kingdom." We would not be gathered here this morning had not Peter and the rest of the apostles finally confessed that the women were right after all.

What message did those women receive? What message did they convey? "Jesus is alive. We have seen him. Christ is risen." It means, "God's love endures forever."

So what? What difference does it make? I am convinced the Easter message means something profound for you and for me. It means the things that get us down, chew us up, and do us in are not the final word. It means the painful, wounding Fridays of our lives may, like that Friday of so long ago, still be called "good." The grief we cannot seem to shake, the sense of failure staring back at us from the ceiling at two in the morning, the near miss that brings tears to our eyes in the funniest places, at the oddest times—all of this rests, finally, in the hands of One who can bear the worst in life with us and, yes, transform us through it to live radiantly, with good humor and abounding hope.

And to be sure, in our lives there is much that gets us down. And there are many ways we can look at those things that get us down. In a reflection from his notebooks, "to be published posthumously," as he says—or after his death, "whichever comes first"—Woody Allen writes:

> Do I believe in God? I did until Mother's accident. She fell on some meat loaf, and it penetrated her spleen. She lay in a coma for months, unable to do anything but sing "Granada" to an imaginary herring. Why was this woman in the prime of her life so afflicted—because in her youth she dared to defy convention and got married with a brown paper bag on her head? And how can I believe in God when just last week I got my tongue caught in the roller of an electric typewriter? I am plagued by doubts. What if everything is an illusion and nothing exists? In that case, I definitely overpaid for my carpet. If only God would give me a clear sign! Like making a large deposit in my name at a Swiss bank.[1]

Chaos, absurdity, no exit—that is one approach to our encounter with the stress and challenge of life.

But there is another approach, and it is born of the Easter gospel. It tackles the worst life does to us, even death itself. I do not suppose many of us have heard of

Charles Lukey. He died a few years ago of a rare terminal disease known as Creutzfeldt-Jakub disease—which is, as one man describes it, "something about a galloping degeneration of the nerve cells." Charles Lukey happened to be the pastor of one of our sibling churches in Middlebury, Connecticut; and when the crisis came, he wrote a letter to his friends, which Sidney Lovett, for many years chaplain at Yale, described as "the most moving credo of Christian faith written in my lifetime." Lukey wrote:

> What does the Christian do when he stands over the abyss of his own death and the doctors have told him that the disease is ravaging his brain and that his whole personality may be warped, twisted, changed? Then, does the Christian have any right to self-destruction, especially when he knows that the changed personality may bring out some horrible beast within himself? Well, after forty eight hours of searching and study, it comes to me that, ultimately and finally, the Christian has to always view life as a gift from God, and see that every precious drop of life was not earned but was a grace, lovingly bestowed on him by his Creator, and it is not his to pick up and smash.
>
> And so, I find the position of suicide untenable, not because I lack the courage to blow out my brains, but rather because of my deep abiding faith in the Creator who put the brains there in the first place. And now the result is that I lie here blind in my bed and trust in the loving, sustaining power of the great Creator who knew and loved me before I was fashioned in my mother's womb. But I do not think it is wrong to pray for an early release from this diseased and ravaged carcass.[2]

"Lovingly given," he closed his statement, "to my congregation and my friends if it seems in good taste."[3] Good taste? What a testimony to the very foundations of the Easter faith and hope; God's love endures forever!

But there is another dimension to it all. It has to do with the Easter defeat of what Paul calls "the rulers, . . . the authorities, . . . the cosmic powers of this present [age]" (Eph. 6:12). On Easter Day we affirm that when God raised Jesus from the dead, the very powers of big religion, big politics, public apathy, imperial orders, nationalistic propaganda, personal complacency, and ambition crucifying Jesus were themselves defeated. God, through the risen Christ, defeats the powers that warp, twist, misdirect, and finally tear human life apart.

To be sure, we live in a world yet resisting that victory. The empty tomb seems mocked by what we see about us. Witness the violence dished out in South Africa. Witness the terror spreading across the Middle East. Witness twenty-one new MX missiles, whose function is to frighten America's antagonists with a perception of overwhelming strength, when in truth they may be a strategic redundancy. Indeed, how many times can you burn Moscow? How many times can you incinerate Boston? Two? Five? A hundred? The more weapons we build, the less secure we are. Therefore, we build more weapons and call it "safety." We slouch toward the militarization of the U.S. economy.

Talk about the structures of death! What does the empty tomb have to say to that? Indeed, what does Easter have to say to all those principalities and powers that seem to get their hold on us and cling tenaciously? Is it really muscle, might, and money that endure forever? Is it national patriotism? Is it the bottom line? Is it career success that claims our energy and our identities, and provides the handles for meaning in our lives? Be careful! For the Easter faith in what truly endures recognizes those things to be transient, deceptive, themselves under the thrall of change and death. The Easter faith in the enduring love of God relocates our loyalties. The Easter faith releases us from knuckling under to, and seeking our ultimate security in, the thing we concoct to save ourselves and

to give life meaning. Easter's revelation of God's enduring love enables us to let go of all those things we
anxiously grasp—our jobs, our nation, our church, our
little causes, survival itself—and letting go of those
things to pronounce with Daniel Berrigan:

> I can only tell you what I believe.
> I believe:
> I cannot be saved by foreign policies.
> I cannot be saved by sexual revolutions.
> I cannot be saved by the gross national product.
> I cannot be saved by nuclear deterrents.
> I cannot be saved by aldermen, priests, artists,
>   plumbers, city planners, social engineers,
>   nor by the Vatican, nor by the World Buddhist
>   Association,
>   nor by angels and archangels nor by powers
>   and denominations.
> I can be saved only by Jesus Christ.[4]

What a difference that faith can make in your life
and mine, and in this world! The freedom born of our
confidence in the conquering reality of Jesus Christ, the
enduring love of God, enables us to encounter this
world with an indefatigable and serene courage. It lib-
erates us to take on the powers that be, the president,
the generals, the mayor, the pope, the minister. It
releases us to tackle the fierce and bitter powers that
would separate us by race, class, gender, nation, or
religion. It frees us to stand, finally, with South Africa's
courageous, faithful bishop, Desmond Tutu, proclaiming
as he did:

> Despite all appearance to the contrary, this is God's
> world. God cares, and cares enormously. His is ulti-
> mately a moral universe that we inhabit, and right
> and wrong matter; and the resurrection of Jesus
> Christ proclaims right will prevail. Goodness and
> love, justice and peace are not illusory, or mirages
> that forever elude our grasp. We must say that Jesus

Christ has inaugurated the Kingdom of God, which
is the Kingdom of Justice, Peace and Love.[5]

We must say it. We must sing it. We must serve it.
We must live it!

Today is Easter
God has raised Jesus from the dead.
You will not find him in a graveyard.
Christ is risen!
God's love endures forever!

3 Can We Live the Easter Hope?

John 20:1-18

Introduction

The Easter emphases mentioned in the introduction to "God's Love Endures Forever" hold for the following sermon as well. A dramatic and radical invasion of human history takes places in the event of Jesus Christ. The event changes, reverses, dissolves the structures and perceptions we live with and under. It helps us to see that what we accept in the routine of our life is unacceptable. John and Paul tend to see "death" as a powerful metaphor for all those things in human life cutting us off from our full humanity, dividing us from one another and setting us over one another. The Easter event proclaims that these old structures we live by are finally dead too, and a new world of mutuality, solidarity, and justice is now and will finally be vindicated.

An empty tomb, abandoned grave clothes, a footrace between rival disciples: we begin there. But John offers more: a woman, a gardener, a bolted room harboring men in terror of the world. John offers the presence of Jesus among them with words, wounds, and a mandate. Some story! What is it about? A ghost? A resuscitated corpse? Is that why we sing and celebrate today—molecules reconstituting themselves? Is that the core of the Easter Hope?

Or does Woody Allen, that savvy, delicious metaphysician, provide our clue to Easter? Remember his notebook reflection?

Once again I tried committing suicide, this time by wetting my nose and inserting it into a light socket. Unfortunately, there was a short in the wiring, and I merely caromed off the icebox. Still obsessed by thoughts of death, I brood constantly. I keep wonder-

45

ing if there is an afterlife; and if there is, will they
be able to break a twenty?[1]

Is that what Easter is all about? Heaven forbid!

In John's story, the Easter Hope means that a new
community confronts the communities we operate in
now. For John himself, writing from a tight, loving
commune, the Easter Hope proclaims a new realm of
mutuality and trust, making its way amid this world of
brokenness and division. John's images tell it all. When
Mary Magdalene turns from the tomb, when she turns
to face Jesus, she fails at recognition. Why? Because
she turns to face a new quality of existence. She looks
at an alternative to life as we know it. She finds it
unrecognizable. When she turns from our world of tombs
and crucifixion, she turns to recognize life, asserting
itself against death.

In truth, she sees Christ as true community. She
comes to realize Christ, not as a resuscitated individ-
ual, but as a new community. She sees One who breaks
through the status quos we structure to kill the likes of
Jesus and fragment the loving, trusting communities
Christ in a new form now embodies. When Mary recognizes the risen Christ, she rejoices in solidarity and
mutuality, she celebrates the embracing of human life
by unconquerable love now asserting itself as victor
over all that would splinter and throw us into chaos.

And yes, there is even more. And it lies at the core
of the Easter message. The Gospel not only provides us
with an announcement about unconquerable love binding us together—reason enough for rejoicing; it challenges us to exercise loving community among ourselves. Easter is not some "mind-boggling" event taking
place in a Palestine garden two thousand years ago.
Easter affirms the ground of our hope today, the root of
our future as a human community. It invites, urges,
draws us to fresh, new ways of treating one another
differently—today, tomorrow, forever.

Can we live, then, this radical Easter Hope? What does it mean for us today? Living the Easter Hope means, first of all, breaking down walls separating us from one another. It affirms that barriers we build, structures we nurture, ideologies we pursue—which cut us off from one another, which marginalize, divide, or in any way thrust human beings into powerless, second-class, personally demeaning circumstances, have no place within the future of God.

Do you remember John's telling us about Jesus confronting those disciples locked in a room against the world? Christ dissolves locked doors. Christ turns closed societies into open societies. To John, Christ brings us the reality of peace through justice.

What a difference the Easter Hope of peace through justice would make in our world, our nation, our city! Only this week, the *New York Times* reported something we all know to be happening in our country: the growing gap between the rich and the poor. From 1979 to 1987, according to the House Ways and Means Committee, the poorest fifth of the nation saw its family income decline by 6.1 percent, while the highest-paid saw theirs increase by 11.1 percent. One congressional representative said, "These trends are inimical to the health of democracy."[2] He is right.

And Boston has not escaped this social disaster. We see the results here in Copley Square. You cannot have avoided reading in the papers these last two years, you cannot have missed seeing on the streets as you walk in this city—perhaps even as you made your way here to church this morning—the terrible consequences of an economic engine running roughshod over the most vulnerable, powerless, and needy in our society. Heaven knows we are familiar with the folk who keep house on the grates over at the library, who sleep in our alley or in the porticos of this very church. But that is the tip of the iceberg.

On a nationwide basis in the last ten years, federal

resources available for housing have decreased from thirty billion to seven billion dollars.³ That is pathetic. That is unconscionable!

In Massachusetts that means in the last five years the number of homeless people in Boston has increased by 26 percent. The number of homeless women and children in Boston has increased by 82 percent.⁴ Half of the kids have developmental problems—they cannot read, write, count; they stay back; they need serious psychiatric help. In the last five years the number of shelters in Massachusetts has increased from seven to ninety. There are three times as many people referred to those shelters as there are beds to handle them. Forty percent of the women referred have been battered.⁵

This represents catastrophic and immoral leadership in a nation and city of astounding wealth. The so-called safety net has collapsed. To be sure, our charity can provide shelters and soup kitchens. Our charity may help people scrape by. Thank heaven for the brilliant and magnanimous contributions of so many in this grave crisis. But churches and private philanthropy barely scratch the surface. Our charity cannot solve this problem.

Do you know why charity cannot solve the problem? Charity seeks to alleviate the immediate need within the confines of the status quo, and it is the status quo that is failing. Charity seldom asks: Why the exponential increase in shelters? Why soup kitchens in a 1989 America whose Administration boasts of the longest-sustained peacetime economic boom in history? Charity does not usually ask the root question: What needs to be changed to bring justice?

That question—the question of justice and what it may mean for taxation, public subsidies, zoning, investment incentives, polling-booth choices, public-policy mandates, constraints on the national obsession that ends up saying, "I'm gonna get mine!" and the bursting of the myth of "trickle down"—this question of justice and solidarity within the human community confronts us at Easter time. Living the Easter Hope means building a community, a city, a nation, a world where locked doors become open doors, where human beings truly live in peace because they live with justice. We will not have a "kinder, gentler nation" without it.

The Easter Hope not only promises peace with justice; it offers each of us a new beginning. It marks a cleansing of community. When the risen Christ stands among those terrified disciples and says, "If you forgive the sins of any, they are forgiven them; if you retain the sins of any, they are retained," he means that by living the Easter Hope we can always begin again with one another. No relationship is so injured, so broken, so mutilated that in the dimensions of unconquerable hope it cannot be re-created.

Heaven knows, most of us need such new beginnings. Our ties to one another are all too tenuous and brittle. We find ourselves in circumstances trying our patience, our tolerance, our goodwill. Many of us can identify with Erma Bombeck, who in trying to hold her family together found herself shouting, "We're going to have some family togetherness here, even if I have to chain you to the bed!"[6]

We live with tensions illustrated by a caustic repartee between George Bernard Shaw and Winston Churchill. Shaw sent Churchill two tickets for the opening night of one of his plays, with the note: "Come and bring a friend—if you have one." Churchill wrote back a regret for opening night, but promised to come the second night, "If there is one."[7]

Sometimes we find ourselves virtually at war with one another. Harry Stein compiled a little book of articles he had written for *Esquire*, and entitled it *Ethics and Other Liabilities*. In it, he tells of a deep-seated resentment that grew between him and his wife, evidencing itself not so much in quarreling, as in ignoring each other. Each was preoccupied with professional problems, far more interested in what was going on in her or his own life than in the other's. Both were angry, he says, and out for retribution. Stein really did not know how bad things were until one afternoon in the country he tauntingly challenged his wife to a footrace, her two laps to his three.

> We began at opposite ends of the yard, and at the signal we took off. It was not until we were within ten feet, both moving at full speed, that it became clear we were going to collide—that in fact, we were engaged in a game of human chicken—and by then it was too late. The impact was awful; both of us collapsed to the ground, and for five minutes we writhed in agony, she clutching her rib cage, I my knee. But at last she looked at me and managed a small smile. "Hey," she said, "let's talk about it."[8]

Yes, as simple, and as difficult, as "talking about it."

Alan Paton, in a memoir written after the death of his wife, Dorrie, remembers a particularly painful occasion when she bluntly told him she could never love him as much as she loved her first husband. Paton, of course, was crushed. But within the mysteries of human relationships and under no small duress, forgiveness was asked for and given; and as he closes his reflection on that occasion, Paton writes:

> What strange creatures we humans are! Just how we come to love one another, and to care for one another for all of our common life, and to grant one another territories on which the other does not trespass, and to bear with one another's foibles and weaknesses, and to grow closer and closer till we have but one mind on all things that matter to us most, and to have children, and to put their welfare and happiness above all other things, and to give them safety and security until it is proper for them to find these things for themselves, how it ever comes to happen in this imperfect world, only God knows.[9]

That is living the Easter Hope: new beginnings, a fresh start, new possibilities for those who live toward Christ's new future.

We need remember that living the Easter Hope has a cost. When John describes Jesus showing wounds to that band of disciples, John illustrates the cost of the Easter Hope. John indicates that those who believe in, and live for, an open society will face tremendous resistance from those who cling to status quos forged by race, sex, privilege, vocation, residence, education. John tells us, frankly, that new beginnings with one another mean passing through pain. You know it. I know it. That is what Good Friday is all about. To live for the new community born of the Easter Hope means that we prepare ourselves at one and the same time for communal joy and also for resistance.

Being ready for this resistance reflects the most encouraging, marvelous, sustaining message Easter brings us. It is captured in a wonderful sermon by Martin Luther King Jr., who paid the cost of the Easter Hope in an effort to build the "beloved community." In a sermon entitled "Our God Is Able," King tells of exhaustion, discouragement, death threats, and, finally, loss of will. King comes to a point where his powers seem exhausted, nothing left, a point where the pending tasks seem overwhelming. Amid this discouragement King tells of an inner transformation and a divine promise: "I will be at your side forever." That promise carried Dr. King through the worst that life could deal out. And so, this morning, I pray that Dr. King's words of assurance become our own as we accept the high privilege, the joy, and the cost of living the Easter Hope:

> When our days become dreary with low-hovering clouds, and our nights become darker than a thousand midnights, let us remember that there is a great, benign power whose name is God; and this power is able to make a way out of no way, and transform dark yesterdays into bright tomorrows.

This is our hope for becoming better women, better men. This is our mandate for seeking to make a better world.[10]

Can you, can I, live the risks and the joy of that Easter Hope? God grant it may be so!

4 Advent's High Calling

Zephaniah 3:14–20

Introduction

Advent provides the churches with their most creative moments. During this marvelous season we are confronted with the promise and reality of the world we hope for. The lectionary passages frequently deal with the apocalyptic visions of the Gospels. They proceed to John the Baptist proclaiming "the way of the Lord" amid a cacophony of voices offering solutions to the human predicament. The lessons from the prophets depict a new kind of community, a polis, a city and world where humankind can live together, sharing a loyalty to Yahweh and serving one another in grace and peace. Advent juxtaposes the realm of God against our realms ruled by greed, power abuse, violence, threat, and force.

Advent comes at us with sharp edges. The Christmas season elicits many memories and emotions, hopes, and feelings among us all. Christmas frequently overwhelms us with sentimentality. The cutting edges of the new world proclaimed by the prophets, anticipated by John, and breaking in among us with the Child of Bethlehem, call us to live in "Christ's new age" by reversing the direction of our lives and turning our priorities upside down and inside out. Advent anticipates a world where economics, politics, and traditional social patterns become transformed by the justice, compassion, and power of God we see in the promise of the Christ-child.

The Divine claims of Advent shake me up no less than they do other people who hear them. They compel a dramatic choice about the kind of life we shall live and the kind of world our faith mandates. The following reflections point toward the kind of world Advent promises—and Christmas affirms.

I always anticipate the Third Sunday of Advent with no little fear and trembling. My personal inclination is to focus on the Advent hope. And in a week like this, where Mikhail Gorbachev's remarkable speech at the United Nations, or the tremendous outpouring of universal concern for earthquake victims in Armenia, captures our attention, a whiff of hope seems to be the order of the day. This week's events give us a sense of the priorities of peace and compassion as we consider our high responsibility and calling in the new world God promises us in Advent.

Nonetheless, the lessons read in churches around the world on this Third Sunday of Advent are not brimming over with hope or goodwill. Indeed, in light of what could be, these lessons begin to see the world as hopeless. That is why I worry about these Advent lessons. In some ways they bear the most devastating, bitter, and enraged outbursts at the human condition we tangle with all year. The passage for this Sunday from the Gospel of Luke, for instance, offers John the Baptist blistering us for betraying God's will. John breathes fire and brimstone at people claiming to be religious and practicing injustice. After assailing ministers and complacent churchgoing types, John heaps fiery furies on extortion, exploitation, and power abuse.

And the Old Testament passages for this Third Sunday of Advent are cut from the same cloth: harsh, extremist, pessimistic in their social and spiritual analysis, terrible in their prescription. Take the prophet Zephaniah, for example. Do you know, in twenty-six years in the Christian ministry I have never chosen to preach from Zephaniah? Do you know why? Because of his furious belief that everything about human life is so rotten it deserves to be wiped out and begun again. I have not preached from Zephaniah because he sees the world in black and white. He sees no good amid the bad, no shades of gray, no noble intentions simply gone awry. He gives no one the benefit of the doubt—no breaks, no second chance, no light at the end of the tunnel. His fury knows no bounds as he proclaims a divine intention to wipe the human slate clean.

Why this fury? Again, like John the Baptist: injustice. And even worse for Zephaniah, complicity by the religious establishment. Zephaniah sees the worst: corrupt judges taking a piece of the action, public life filled with the brazen search for gain at the price of the truth. Zephaniah sees money-grubbing without a second glance at who gets lost in the shuffle, thrown into the street, dumped on the social scrap heap. And the ministers, he says, go on planning their Advent services, hiding in their studies, going to their Christmas parties, while terrible things happen to human beings and the world seems to be falling apart.

It is this outrage at religious complacency in the face of greed, social indifference, and official sleaze that fires Zephaniah's polemic. He directs his fury at what he calls

> the people
> who rest complacently on their dregs,
> those who say in their hearts,
> "The LORD will not do good,
> nor will he do harm"
> —Zephaniah 1:12

Do you know what Zephaniah means by that? I am almost afraid to tell you. As one brilliant expositor, George Adam Smith, writes:

> The metaphor is clear. New wine was left upon its lees [that is, upon its sediment or dregs] only long enough to fix its colour and body. If not then drawn off it grew thick and syrupy—sweeter, indeed, than the strained wine, and to the taste of some, more pleasant, but feeble and ready to decay.[1]

Are you beginning to get a feel for Zephaniah's point? Zephaniah rails, says Smith, against

the criminal apathy of well-to-do people sunk in ease
and religious indifference. . . . The great causes of
God and Humanity are not defeated by the hot as-
saults of the Devil, but by the slow, crushing, glacier-
like mass of thousands and thousands of indifferent
nobodies. God's causes are never destroyed by being
blown up, but by being sat upon. It is not the violent
and the anarchical whom we have to fear in the war
for human progress, so much as the slow, the staid,
the respectable. And the danger of these does not lie
in their stupidity. Notwithstanding their religious
profession, it lies in their skepticism. Respectability
may be the precipitate of unbelief. Nay, it is that,
however religious its mask, wherever it is mere comfort, decorousness and conventionality; where, though
it would abhor articulately confessing that God does
nothing, it virtually means so—*says* so (as Zephaniah puts it) *in its heart* by refusing to share the
manifest opportunities of serving [God], and covers
its sloth and fear by hinting that God is not with the
great crusades for freedom . . . to which it is sum-
moned. What makes mere respectability so dangerous is that like the unshaken, unstrained wine to
which the prophet compares its obscure and muddy
comfort, it tends to decay.[2]

And Zephaniah is not done. Those of us, so to speak,
"thickening on our lees," will be "searched out with
lights," our sloth, cowardice, and indifference exposed.
No one of us will escape because we have said,
"Everybody's doing it," or "Who can fight city hall?" or
"Let George do it." "We shall be followed and judged,
each of us for his or her personal attitude to the move-
ments of our time. These things are not too high for us:
they are *our* duty; and we cannot escape by slinking
into the shadow."[3]

Hear that? It shakes me up! Has Zephaniah put a
finger on you, on me, on our church?

I am not going to leave you there, because Zephaniah does not. After all his polemics, threats, the fury

at complacency, he does close with a word of hope and opportunity. It feels like a non sequitur. But finally Zephaniah does sound an authentic note of Advent hope and responsibility. He promises, in the first place, a new era, a new time, a new creation grounded in love and justice, where the barriers are down, where, under God, we are the human family. "There's a new world coming," the prophet sings. He is upbeat. So far, so good.

But more: that new creation shakes us out of our complacency. Remember, Zephaniah is furious at our failure to serve God faithfully. To Zephaniah, all our achievements ring hollow against what he sees as our most crucial human problem: how we treat other people, how we enter the lists—or fail—to exercise mercy, compassion, justice. Someone of more recent vintage than Zephaniah makes Zephaniah's point. Robert Kennedy remarked, "Each time someone stands up for an ideal or acts to improve the lot of others or strikes out against injustice, that person sends forth a tiny ripple of hope."[4]

Got it? Sending forth tiny ripples of hope: what a marvelous, glorious vocation that is! That is what our disturbing prophet believes we are to be and to do. That is Advent's high calling.

PART TWO

Economic and Social Justice

5 Homeless

John 1:1–14

Introduction

Some time ago a colleague of mine greeted me on the street with the line, "Well, Jim, I see you work in the high-rent district now." He is right, of course. The Old South Church in Boston is located in Boston's Back Bay. Over the last ten or fifteen years the neighborhood has changed dramatically. "Baby boomers" made their way to the brick row-house housing stock, an enormous Government expenditure of defense contracting money made its way into Massachusetts technology companies, the computer revolution drew capital and people, private development with public incentives broadened the tourist industry. The Back Bay, the South End, Beacon Hill became "gentrified." And to a great degree the constituencies in the churches reflected the demographics of the neighborhood.

So what might Christmas be all about to this successful and enterprising constituency? How remind them (and myself) that the One who comes to us at Christmastime resides outside the pale of the "high-rent district"? How confront this congregation and myself with this visitor from "another world," who came among us with none of the accoutrements and security most of us seek, if not possess? By telling the Christmas story, of course. By reminding a congregation that a social problem afflicting the city of Boston afflicted our Savior. By interpreting for them anew the elements of the birth of a "homeless" one and how that story could be ours.

The reader will note in the Postscript to this book a number of efforts initiated by Old South to alleviate in a tiny degree the massive housing problem in Boston. The church set up a housing office in an effort to engage church members, to leverage assets, to join in ecumenical efforts to bring some housing on line in the city. Over the years the church trustees have co-signed loans with community organizations, they have invested at below-market interest rates in community loan funds, they have joined with others in providing capital for significant housing initiatives in Boston.

The problem is not solved. As the nineties begin it appears to be even more grave. Unquestionably, church people and their institutions will be called on to participate in the alerting of public officials to the problem and in providing resources for its alleviation.

A great window dominates the front of our sanctuary. Different sectors of the window depict the events surrounding the birth of Jesus. The heavenly host announce the Messiah's coming. The shepherds bow in anticipation. As you look at it, you can see the star in the upper left-hand corner. Above this great scene, in a special constellation of windows, you can spot the crèche, the Madonna, Joseph, and the Christ-child. Whatever else happens in this great old building, the announcement of Christ Jesus' coming into our world confronts us week in and week out.

But I wonder. I wonder if those of us who encounter Christmas, week in and week out, through this window—I wonder if we see and hear this message afresh? Indeed, are we open to receive the new world of Christ Jesus announced by this glorious window, our cards, our carols, and, on Christmas Eve, our candlelight?

I ask these questions because John, that most profound of the Evangelists, includes two striking allusions as he begins his reflection on the meaning of Jesus:

> The Word was in the world, and the world was made through the Word, yet the world did not know the Word. The Word came to the Word's own home, but those to whom the Word came did not receive the Word.
>
> —John 1:10–11 (AILL)

Why not? I believe the Christmas event, for all our magnificent Christmas windows and beautiful cards, provokes a crisis of recognition. I believe that what most of us hope for in a Savior is not what we get. I believe that what we look for, what we expect, what we want in a Christ blinds us frequently to the Christ who really comes. And I am persuaded those of us in the

Christian ministry are among the most sadly deceived. *"The Word came to the Word's own home, but those to whom the Word came did not receive the Word. The Word was in the world, . . . yet the world did not know the Word."* The Word, even Jesus Christ, comes to us as stranger, as outsider—as one with no place to lay his head. He seeks a home among us, but cannot find one.

This strange, homeless Jesus pervades the New Testament's perspective. The Gospels illustrate it from the very beginning: no acceptance, no security, no home. Luke makes reference to it when he tells us bluntly Jesus came into the world in a stable because there was no room for him at the inn. But Matthew offers us an even more vivid account. That splendid narrative we read year after year—about the magi following the star, their arrival at the manger, their offering of gold, frankincense, and myrrh—is couched in a story telling of Herod's outright rejection. Herod sends those magi as informers, as personal spies. No sooner is Jesus born in the outbuildings of a Bethlehem inn than his family flees the country. "Into the wild and painful cold of the starless winter night came the refugees slowly making their way to the border," writes the poet.[1]

We see the husband with his wife and child, dodging border patrols, sustaining silence, wandering in circles in the bleak desert night. That is how Jesus spent the first years of his life: on the run, homeless. *"The Word came to the Word's own"* and they failed to recognize the Word.

And we find this crisis not only at Jesus' birth; his life and ministry engage us with One who seems uneasy among us. His parables, for instance, confront us with a world so different from the one we support with our taxes, a world so different from the imperialism, militarism, and greed we nourish and encourage—a world so different as to be virtually unrecognizable. Jesus tells the parable of the good Samaritan to national chauvinists, ethnic elites, political and religious insiders who believe their closed circles to be special, who see no good coming from beyond their tastes and class. "Who is my neighbor?" they ask, convinced she will look like them. What neighbor does Jesus give them? A Samaritan—an enemy, an outsider, an alien, one whom they consider foreign in their own land— comes and saves that "insider" lying in the ditch, when those who *look* like that insider, *think* like him, *speak* like him, *pray* like him, pass right by. That parable falls on the stunned and unbelieving ears of those unable to embrace saving truth outside themselves.

And if Jesus' birth and ministry illustrate his homelessness among us, what really lies behind his death? Could it be an inability to fit him into categories or to house him in a way we believe to be appropriate? He defies containment in orthodox dogmas or institutions. He refuses to indulge in our religious sentimentality. And for church and state, Jesus will not surrender his loyalty to the imperial designs of the oligarchs. In his own time, Jesus triggered a committee on unorthodox and anti-Roman activities. The verdict? Death to the atheist. Death to the traitor. "The Word came to the Word's own," and was unrecognized, driven into a far country, refused a home.

Does John's observation strike a note with us? Whom do we expect in Advent? What do we want at Christmas? Do we want an insider, somebody who speaks our language, responds to our hopes, feeds our dreams— someone we recognize as our own, a friend we would invite for cider and cheese? Perhaps. But mark this well: this Christ—

who offers salvation through outsiders;
who hangs around with the ne'er-do-wells from
    nowhere;
who began life headed for the border;
of the foreign Samaritan;
of the cross beyond the city;
the one born outside the inn—

this Jesus Christ at Christmastime comes again to this world, this city, this church, your life and mine—and seeks a home.

And I worry. I worry because among us this Christ may again be homeless. In a world where power, money, guns, success, connections, and credentials rule the roost—in such a world weakness, poverty, service, solidarity with the failed, the vulnerable, the prisoners, become laughable, a joke, a mistake, unrecognizable as anything but a losing cause. But is it a losing cause?

> God has shown strength with God's arm;
>   God has scattered the proud in the thoughts of
>   their hearts.
> God has brought down the powerful from
>   their thrones,
>   and lifted up the lowly;
> God has filled the hungry with good things,
>   and sent the rich away empty.
>   —Luke 1:51–53

Luke puts those words in Mary's mouth as she anticipates birth.

Or again, in a society where we determine personal identities by grade-point average, office location, niche in the church hierarchy, by our income, our fragrance, or our automobile logo, in such a society can we find a home for identities rooted in love, embracing the marginal, the failure, the fringe, the lonely, the misfit, the homeless? Can we, as Simone Weil asks, "remain in a sense anonymous, ever ready to be mixed into the common paste of humanity?"[2] That is where Jesus, whom we call Christ, comes to us: in the "common paste of humanity"—no place, no home for a real Christ, but in hope, and in love, the only home.

Michel Quoist puts Christ's homelessness and its dilemma for us poignantly:

Lord, why did you tell me to love [my brothers and
   sisters]?
I have tried, but I come back to you, frightened. . . .

Lord, I was so peaceful at home, I was so comfortably
   settled.
It was well-furnished, and I felt cozy.
I was alone, I was at peace,
Sheltered from the wind and the rain, kept clean.
I would have stayed unsullied in my ivory tower.
But, Lord, you have discovered a breach in my defenses.
You have forced me to open my door.
Like a squall of rain in the face, [human cries have]
   awakened me;
Like a gale of wind a friendship has shaken me,
Stealing in like a shaft of light, your grace has disturbed me.
Rashly enough, I left my door ajar. Now, Lord, I am lost!
Outside, men [and women] were lying in wait for me.
I did not know they were so near; in this house, in
   this street, in this office; my neighbor, my colleague,
   my friend.
As soon as I started to open the door I saw them, with
   outstretched hands, anxious eyes, longing hearts, like
   beggars on church steps.

The first came in, Lord. There was, after all, a bit of space
   in my heart.
I welcomed them. I would have cared for them and fondled
   them, my very own little lambs, my little flock.
You would have been pleased, Lord; I would have served and
   honored you in a proper, respectable way.
Until then; it was sensible. . . .
But the next ones, Lord, the [others], I had not seen them;
   they were hidden behind the first ones.
There were more of them. They were wretched; they
   overpowered me without warning.
We had to crowd in, I had to find room for them.

Now they have come from all over in successive waves,
   pushing one another, jostling one another.
They have come from all over town, from all parts of the
   country, of the world; numberless, inexhaustible.

They don't come alone any longer, but in groups, bound
   one to another.
They come bending under heavy loads; loads of injustice,
   of resentment and hate, of suffering and sin. . . .
They drag the world behind them, with everything rusted,
   twisted, badly adjusted.

Lord, they hurt me! They are in the way, they are all over.
They are too hungry; they are consuming me!
I can't do anything any more; as they come in, they push the
   door, and the door opens wider. . . .
Ah, Lord! My door is wide open!
I can't stand it any more! It's too much! It's no kind of a life!
   What about my job?
   My family?
   My peace?
   My liberty?
   Ah, And me?
Ah, Lord, I have lost everything; I don't belong to myself any
   longer;
There's no more room for me at home.

Don't worry, God says, you have gained all,
While men [and women] came in to you,
I, your Father,
I, your God,
Slipped in among them.*

This world, this city, your heart and mine are most
truly the home of this Christmas child. Jesus Christ is
not meant to be homeless here. No one is meant to be
homeless here. The great Christmas challenge before
each of us is to create a world where Jesus Christ can
be at home anywhere—a world secured not by class
and income, but by love and justice; a world sustained
not by pecking orders and dog-eat-dog competition, but
by reconciliation and mutual service; a world bound by

*From "Lord, Why Did You Tell Me To Love?" in *Prayers* by Michel
Quoist, trans., Agnes M. Forsyth and Ann Marie de Commaille (Kansas City, Mo.: Sheed & Ward, 1963). Used by permission of the
publisher.

our solidarity with one another and with our so-called enemies; a world grounded by faith that amid our chaos and broken dreams there throbs Love risking herself among us, ready to take whatever we dish out and, yes, never letting us go. The world where this Christ-child may finally lay his head is the world where they wander in our alley, where the "wino" on the Blagden Street grates, the vagrant leaning on our wall, the Ethiopian, the Palestinian, the Salvadoran, the Russian Jew finally has a place to lay his head, to rest her feet, to live in hope, in joy, in peace. It is the kind of world where our restless lives and troubled hearts find a haven. The Bethlehem refugee invites us to design and build that kind of world.

Can we accept the invitation? Can we work for a true homecoming this Christmastime? God grant that it may be so.

6 The Gospel Confronts Us with a Claim Over Life and Death

Mark 5:21–43

Introduction

In a series of sermons delivered during Lent, 1988, the theme focused on Christ's "decisive encounters." One of those encounters includes a woman with an incurable flow of blood. Her condition and the stigma it bore in Jesus' time enabled me to approach the AIDS pandemic and its implications for the exercise of the gospel in our time.

And surely the presence of AIDS continues to haunt and threaten all of us. Every day something new about its spread, its victims, its antidotes appears in major news stories. The public discussion reveals not only enormous scientific and medical import, it bears serious political and human rights issues as well. AIDS patients find themselves increasingly isolated from society. Many suffer not only the personal trauma and isolation associated with the disease, they also happen to be identified with lifestyles, cultural and ethnic roots, and sexual orientations resisted, if not spurned, by the larger society.

Churches have become increasingly sensitive to the delicate yet overwhelming constellation of issues emanating from the AIDS crisis. Denominations, ecumenical agencies, and interfaith grass-roots associations are tackling legislative advocacy, personal care, and attitudinal change. Congregational members are acquainted with individuals or the families of individuals who, from whatever source, have contracted the HIV virus. In many cities healing services are held on a regular basis. Intercessory prayer and words of hope are the order of the day.

This goes on at Old South too. Church members and staff participate in an AIDS ministry. It includes regular gathering for prayer and encourages pastoral care for AIDS patients. Recently, in memory of one of its employees, a corporation made a significant contribution to the Old South for support of its AIDS ministry. The ameliorating of this plague is a task far larger than our churches can handle. Yet, somehow, we can remind the world and one another that though we may not possess the clues to curing AIDS, we can surely promote healing. We can assist those afflicted and their loved ones in the process of reconciliation with a God who will not let anything separate them from the Divine grace and love.

Jesus comes back home from visiting in foreign territory. He is immediately met by two people in terrible trouble. The first is a religious official whose daughter has been stricken. The second is a woman suffering from an unstoppable flow of blood. For twelve years she has lived with this affliction. She wants to be rid of it. Seeing Jesus, she decides to make a move. Perhaps by touching the hem of his garment she will be healed.

Clearly the woman finds herself reluctant to speak with Jesus. I see her coming out of the shadows— hesitant, veiled, hiding her infirmity. Mark tells of her desperation. She has sought out every glimmer of help, indulged in every cure. She has followed the advice of what might be the first-century equivalents of gynecologists, oncologists, hematologists, pharmacologists, psychiatrists, hypnotists, acupuncturists, gurus, biofeedback experts, chiropractors, health-food advisors, and televangelist healers—not to mention a library of self-help books, attitudinal refresher courses, homemade remedies, and a trip to an exotic spa. And, as Mark tells us, the blood flow has stemmed not one whit. Indeed, she has only grown worse.

Can we tell what disease afflicted her? Who knows. Clearly she suffered a chronic illness virtually impossible to heal. Perhaps in our time it might be treated with a simple medication or a surgical procedure. We can speculate about the biomedical aspects of her condition. No doubt there exists a sizable literature in the commentaries dealing with the pathology of her illness.

But I do not think Mark's interest lies first of all in the details of the woman's medical history. I think he writes about meanings. I think Mark tries to deal with the implications of her illness for her life, her identity, her social relationships. I think Mark tries to express the meaning of her plight for his own Christian community and its perception, through Jesus, of what God wants for human life. I believe Mark offers us this narrative not to boggle us with a smashing medical miracle. He offers us this incident in order to touch us with the dimensions of what it means to be a human being, sustained, embraced, included in the blessed family of God as revealed through the humanity of Jesus Christ.

We begin for a moment with the woman. What does this chronic affliction mean for her? How does she perceive herself? How is she perceived by others? We catch a glimpse of the answer in her secretive, desperate approach to Jesus.

First of all, she comes as a woman. In the first century, that means she comes as a second-class citizen. In a society in every way giving preference to men she represents the "disprivileged," the marginalized, the disinherited.[1]

Secondly, she comes to Jesus impoverished. She has spent "all that she had" on treatment from many doctors. Her poverty exacerbates her marginality, her existence amid disprivilege.[2]

And, yes, she comes with this chronic illness, this unstemmed flow of blood. The illness does not simply discomfit her; the illness, as understood by her compatriots, means she is polluted, unsavory. She lives where one of the basic religious tenets found in the Torah reads like this:

> If a woman has a discharge of blood for many days, not at the time of her impurity, or if she has a discharge beyond the time of her impurity, all the days of the discharge she shall continue in uncleanness; as in the days of her impurity, she shall be unclean. Every bed on which she lies during all the

days of her discharge shall be treated as the bed of her impurity; and everything on which she sits shall be unclean, as in the uncleanness of her impurity. Whoever touches these things shall be unclean.

—Leviticus 15:25–27

Now, friends, we can all see the distortions in this law. We recognize the injustice: the outrageous, brutal, unfair, blind, inhuman gender discrimination lying at the root of this Levitical decree. That someone should believe God stands behind it makes it even more abhorrent. But that is our twentieth-century assessment. In the first century this Levitical tenet reflects and determines cultural, personal, and religious reality. The woman's crippling illness marks her as a blighted human being. She is perceived and perceives herself as impaired humanity. Her illness means she is defective, she is tainted, she is flawed. She is not simply among the "disprivileged" as a woman, she is not only among the disinherited through her poverty; she suffers a debilitating, painful, chronic illness that signifies a shame, a disgrace, a humiliation—a stigma no less wounding, painful, and debilitating than her illness. In social terms, she is an outcast. In religious terms she is God-damned.

Can the woman's wound be healed, her stigma purged? That question confronts Mark and his little church. In the face of everything around him saying no, Mark says, "In the name of the love of Christ, such a person can be—is—restored." When that woman with her chronic illness and its demeaning consequences touches the hem of Jesus' garment; when she dares open herself to the possibilities of acceptance, restoration, and healing; when she risks approaching the love she tremulously hopes will embrace even her; she finds, in and through the love of God in Mark's church, her faith vindicated. The barriers do collapse, her stigma dissolves, her wound heals, her full humanity is affirmed. The love breaking through everything reaches even her, bringing with it healing, reconciliation, wholeness.

A great story? Yes. A marvelous testimony? To be sure. Does it bear an insight and challenge for our own time, to you, to me, to our churches? I think it does at any number of points. Today, we just try one. I am worried, friends. Like Mark and the threatening impact of that hemorrhaging woman, I am worried about the impact of AIDS on the fabric of church and society. I worry, not only because of AIDS' devastating and finally terminal impact on those who bear the disease— that seems awful enough—but I worry because AIDS bears social and moral dimensions of such horrendous scope. AIDS is not simply a disease we seek to cure with elite scientists, laboratories, and millions for research. Would that it were so simple.

No, this illness, like the illness Mark describes in that wounded and suffering woman, carries questions striking at and threatening the roots of our humanity. AIDS calls into question and threatens the very heart of our identities, the solidarity of human community, the depths of our compassion—how we treat one another. AIDS is a virus threatening not only the biological tissue of individuals, but the social tissue binding us together. As we seek to manage AIDS, to control AIDS, to treat AIDS, to live and succor and bear with those who contract AIDS, we will discover, as Mark made so clear in his narrative of the woman with the hemorrhage—we will discover the fissures, the injustices, the inhumanities, the fears, the outright terror and contempt we hold for one another. We will confront the dehumanization of stigma rooted in illness, the breaking of moral conventions, or the aberration from social propriety. Our commitment to a human family under God will undergo, and is even now undergoing, severe testing. We will have to fight AIDS with every weapon of compassion and concern, every measure of hard evidence, truth, and love we can muster.

Look at just some of the issues this morning. Across the country, about two thirds of AIDS patients are male homosexuals or bisexuals. In Massachusetts, as of December 1987, homosexual and bisexual males constituted nearly 70 percent of the cases.[3] Already stigmatized and separated, already considered "other" and "outsider"—on top of all that they have an illness bearing the certainty of death! Talk about fissures, wounds, stigmata!

Arthur Kleinman, in a marvelous book entitled *The Illness Narratives*, interviews a thirty-two-year-old teacher whom he pseudonymously names Horacio Grippa. Mr. Grippa, writes Kleinman, was a young man who happened to be a homosexual. He was about to leave the hospital, his life in disarray. When his AIDS was revealed he was fired from his job, his landlord demanded he vacate his apartment, his parents locked him out of the house, his medical insurance company hedged on his medical bills. "The nurses are scared of me," he said. "The doctors wear masks and sometimes gloves. Even the priest doesn't seem too anxious to shake my hand. What the hell is this? I am not a leper. Do they want to stand me up and shoot me? I've got no family, no friends. Where do I go? What do I do? God, this is terrible. Is God punishing me? The only thing I've got going for me is that I'm not dying—at least not yet."[4]

We know church and society face one of their most deep-seated identity crises right here. As William Sloane Coffin asks rhetorically, "Can anyone doubt that if the primary group of victims had been upper-middle-class heterosexual whites, funding from the government . . . would have been ten times what it is today?"[5] Question: Where will gay men and lesbian women, already suffering the wounds of social separation, now doubly stigmatized by illness, discover the healing that Jesus offered that bleeding, outcast woman in similar circumstances? Could it be here?

Or again, Ellen Goodman recently wrote of Lorraine Day, chief of orthopedics at the San Francisco General Hospital. Dr. Day goes into the operating room, writes Goodman, in "full protective gear. Two pairs of gloves, goggles, a face mask, double sleeves, double shoe covers, boots up to her knees." Goodman tells us Dr. Day is scared and not a little angry. Comments Dr. Day,

> Yesterday, I did five operations. Thirty percent of my patients are at high risk for AIDS. One of my patients recently needed two hundred fifty pints of blood. It was pouring into him and all over us. They tell us to be careful. But as a surgeon, you cut yourself many times. Would you tell a carpenter, "Don't cut yourself for the rest of your life?" . . . Honestly, I have to decide whether I want to continue in medicine.[6]

What troubles Dr. Day? Well, no one can tell her whether or not her patient carries the AIDS virus. Why? Because the information is not a simple biomedical fact. It invades the most private and personal aspects of our lives. It is information bearing, perhaps, traumatic consequences. It could indicate, against the deepest wishes of the patient, the patient's homosexuality, bisexuality, or drug problems. It could threaten a patient's ties to his spouse, his family, his job. It is a terrible bind, for although the evidence indicates the risks to Dr. Day are effectively nil, she still fears for her life. What to do? The question exacerbates a health-care problem already evidenced. As reported in a recent issue of the *Village Voice*:

> In a recent survey of nine hundred doctors in California (which has more AIDS cases than any state except New York), 39 percent said they felt "some-

times" or "often" uncomfortable in treating homosexual patients. The study found a correlation between homophobia and competence in treating people with AIDS. The authors conclude, "A significant proportion of primary-care physicians throughout California, including those in the two largest metropolitan areas, cannot be expected to appropriately diagnose, counsel, or refer patients at high risk of AIDS."[7]

California may be an exception, but I do not think so. Our most treasured assumptions about medical care, about doctors and patients—their perception, their trust, and their confidence in one another—are seriously threatened by this virus. God grant that healing may take place among the healers.

A recent article appeared in the *Christian Century*, entitled "We Are the Church with AIDS."[8] The article centers on San Francisco's Metropolitan Community Church, a congregation of gay men and lesbian women in the heart of the city. The article chronicles the men and women in the congregation who carry the virus and suffer with it; it tells of those who know, who love, and who grieve for the sick and the dying.

As I read the article, it occurred to me the Metropolitan Community churches are not the only ones with AIDS. All our churches could well say, "We are the church with AIDS." Loved ones among us may right now carry, or in the future may carry, the AIDS virus. In our congregation are any number of health-care professionals who tend patients, their families, friends, or lovers through the long ordeal. One of them told me just the other day she developed a peculiar and unique attachment to her AIDS patients. Others of us will be forced to reevaluate our most intimate relationships. We will be compelled to decide, discuss, and act on matters of public policy we thought reserved for only the most private domains. Shall we allow addicts to trade old IV needles for new ones at public expense? Shall we test—and if so, whom, how, and when—for the virus? We will see sex education not simply as a personal and family matter, but as an up-front, bold-lettered issue of public health and disease control.

Each of us will stand at the bedside, and eventually at the grave, of someone we worked with, lived with, or admired, who through sexual contact, blood transfusion, a shared needle, or birth transmission will succumb to this disease. AIDS will become a reference, an illustration, the backdrop of countless sermons and prayers. And just like that congregation of Mark's, faced by the illness and stigma of that wounded woman, we will be faced with deciding how we shall respond to those stigmatized by the world at large with this terrible illness and all it might indicate about their identities. Make no mistake about it. It is not a matter of us and them, our churches and their churches, the normal and the blemished. We are the church of the hemorrhaging woman. We are the church with AIDS.

But more wonderfully and paradoxically, I believe we can be also the hem of Jesus' garment. My fondest hope is that in this Christian community each of you may be seen, loved, and embraced through whatever your own woundedness for the rich, deep, glorious human being you are. My prayer is that here in this congregation the barriers, labels, phobias, prejudices, and stigmas separating us may dissolve. Can it happen? Dare we risk it? Does the suffering, overflowing love of God saturate this place? Brother, sister, in the words of the gospel, I pray, open yourself among us. Go in peace and be healed.

7 Crowned with Glory and Honor

Introduction

Who attends church on Sunday morning? In our church one can find large numbers of young men and women born in those crucial years between 1946 and 1964—the men and women of the baby boom. They come to Boston because they go to school here or because, after graduating, they find good jobs and thousands of young people their own age to work and to play with.

A significant change has occurred among this generation, however, especially among women. There is a dramatic difference between their self-identity and, in most cases, that of their mothers. In one generation domestic relationships, workplace structures, cultural roles, and expectations have altered in ways no doubt dreamed of, but seldom believed possible. Equal rights, equal status, equal privileges, all the qualities and components of human self-realization, became the order of the day. Broad assumptions concerning identity and role were turned upside down and inside out.

The church is no less affected by the tremendous urge for change. Traditionally, the church's attitudes, vocabulary, and symbols for ultimate reality led to ecclesial structures defining women as "second-class citizens." The great female metaphors for God were overcome by male metaphors. By accepting without question the usual male symbols and metaphors for God, the faithful assumed the very foundations of human existence rested on hierarchies reflecting male dominance.

Time for a change. But how? Well, in order to begin perceptual change and still to maintain the core of Christian faith, religious language and its symbolic freight has become a center of contention in the churches. Male metaphors for God are not adequate. The search for, and use of, an increasing number of metaphors for God is the order of the day. The emergence of female metaphors for God brings diversity and plays to a broader and deeper imagery for the ineffable God. This occurs, of course,

79

in preaching, in prayers, in hymnody. The effort causes no small controversy in seminaries and in local churches.

The Old South Church in Boston is not immune to the controversy. Congregants furious with "bowdlerized" hymns and recast scripture make themselves known and felt. Those sympathetic to the changes offer friendly encouragement. Many, of course, are simply bewildered by it all.

Nonetheless, the church has a subgroup of the deacons continuing to look at the matter of inclusive language. We find ourselves increasingly unable to use many of the hymns in one of the classic hymnals of its time, the *Pilgrim Hymnal*. We read from the *An Inclusive-Language Lectionary*, we alter texts, we change classics. For the sake of the gospel, we seek human equality.

Who is God? Who are we? For religious people, those two questions are inextricably related. What we believe about God ultimately determines what we believe about the nature and quality of human life. And what we believe about human life often determines how we conceive of, and how we serve, the primary loyalty of our life—that ultimate sovereignty we call God. The issues confront us every day of our lives: "How shall I use my money?" "What shall I do about my sick mother?" "What must I do to get so-and-so to love me?" Not to mention the issues perplexing and dividing our communities: What or who determines a woman's choice about her pregnancy? What is the basis for the state's decision to end a life by lethal injection? Where shall we stand when a nation, in God's name, believes in and practices apartheid? These questions, and others like them, link our loyalty to God with what we believe about ourselves and human life.

All of which brings us to our psalm for the morning, probably the greatest of all the creation psalms. It is a hymn of praise written during a time of national and religious prosperity, thanking God for making the times good times, and understanding the best in human life— your life and mine—as well as our responsibility on this earth to be like that of the king the psalmist knew—

Saul or David or Solomon—a ruler in charge of history and nature. As the psalmist says:

> You have given [us] dominion over the works of
>   your hands;
> you have put all things under [our] feet.
>   —Psalm 8:6

This psalm, and the thinking behind it, probably played no small part in Western civilization's march to conquer the earth, to master its resources, to conceive of its forests and minerals, its water, energy, and atmosphere as made for us to unlock and to use for our own ends. This psalm is the capitalist's dream and the ecologist's nightmare. It reflects on our stewardship of God's earth, of our resources, of one another.

Yet, rather than speaking directly to this stewardship theme, what I want to do this morning is to focus on the great prologue (Ps. 8:1, 4, AILL):

> O SOVEREIGN, our God,
>   how majestic is your name in all the earth!

I want to focus on that, as well as on the question:

> What are human beings that you are mindful
>   of them,
> and mortals that you care for them?

Indeed, I want to focus on the questions, Who is this majestic God? and, Who are we that this God is mindful of us? These questions lie not only behind the psalmist's glorious answer—that God is like a royal steward, and so are we—but also behind the psalms, the hymns we sing here, the prayers we say, the scriptures we read, the confessions we make—the very way we talk about, perceive, and picture the God whom we worship and serve. It is in an attempt to tackle these questions, Who is God? and, Who are we? that we include in our bulletin, from time to time, hymns that appear bowdlerized, scriptures that deviate from the way we are used to hearing them, ascriptions for God that are unusual. We are trying to tackle the questions that confront a living people, encountering a living God in every age: God, who are you? Who are we? What are you like? How can we talk about you? Do our answers make any difference in how we perceive and treat one another?

Finding answers to these questions is, of course, the task of every culture, every church, every Christian, in every time. That is why we write new prayer books, assemble new hymnals. That is why some people get into trouble with their bishops, tangle with a pope, or get condemned by an ecclesiastical council. That is why I do not preach the same sermon every week, why my library tends to grow, and why continual discussion flows within the life of the church. God is not static; neither is human life.

This ever-continuing task of perceiving, of describing, of relating this majestic God of ours to human life has been given a peculiar urgency in our time and in our churches by women. What are women saying? Why this urgency? What is going on? And what does it mean for our perennial task of interpreting, committing our loyalty to, and serving God and God's children, wherever and whoever they be?

The urgency arises from many sources and has many ramifications. But first of all it seems to me to be a matter of the fullness of women's humanity. Whoever denied that? Well, friends, sadly enough our own religious tradition has been one of the worst offenders. How? I mean that the criteria for judgments about what makes a human being human have been made throughout history primarily by men. Human perceptions tending, as they do, to tilt toward the self-interest of those who make them, the definitions of full humanity have tended to tilt toward the strengths we associate with men.

What are these supposed strengths? We perceive them as virtues: autonomy, courage, fairness, winning in adversarial relationships, sticking up for principles, decisive action, facing down the enemy, defeating the forces of nature. In addition, ruling in royal fashion the universe, the nation, and the household have been the basic marks against which a full humanity is measured. They are ostensibly the virtues of the real world.

And the virtues we associate with women: empathy, compassion, connectionalism, caring, nurture, reluctance to choose standing up for an abstract principle if it means doing an injury—all these virtues, while appreciated and given their due, when laid against the male virtues are seen by many of us as, well, maybe a little naive or sentimental. Women's virtues in the realm of tough decisions, power plays, war and peace, and the marketplace are seen as perhaps immature, inadequate for life's true tests. The gifts and virtues that tend to predominate in women are seen in general as weaker, softer, less tangible than the gifts that tend to predominate in men. They are seen that way partly because it is men, in general, who succeed in publishing the psychology, the history, the sociology, and much of the poetry and fiction. It is men who preach the sermons, compose and ratify many of the religious texts of humankind. There simply is a male bias written into the very marrow of our perceptions and institutions.

Now, some women down the centuries have said no to that bias. They have said no to the perceptions and institutions sustaining it. And today, women are saying no again. To what? Women are saying no to the way we Christians talk, and sing, and pray about the most meaningful things in our lives: God, and what God wants for us. The way we Christians talk and what it means for our common life are vulnerable to the accusation that our understanding of the orders of creation continues to confirm a secondary role and place for women in those orders.

How could we do such a thing? One way we do it is by continuing to express and confess our perception that the universe is ruled by a God for whom the most adequate metaphor is male: "King," "Lord," "Father," "He," "Him." Those metaphors, as wonderful, cherished, and legitimate as they may be, cannot contain all of who God is. But by using them most of the time, we tend to affirm a creation founded and rooted in a hierarchy with—at least as the psalmist and much of the Bible see it—a figurative king at the top.

With these usual masculine metaphors for God we are saying that creation, the universe, and reality as we confess it are dominated finally by a sovereign whose divine attributes are mostly male, and for whom the lesser orders—the nation, the church, the family, the workplace—are but earthly models. In the scriptures, hymns, and confessions that we frequently recite, and which Christians have offered together for centuries, we are saying, simply: men are in charge; male hegemony is built into the order of things. That is the way God wants it.

Is it really the way God wants it? You see, we are not just fiddling around with words. We are fiddling around with the very things the words point to. We are fiddling around with reality itself. Take the hymn, for example: "I Sing the Mighty Power of God." The first stanza contains the line:

"The moon shines full at *his* command."

In *Inclusive Language Hymns* the line reads:

"The moon shines full at *God's* command."

Or in the third stanza, Watts wrote:

"And everywhere that *man* can be."

That reference to "man" just does not work. It excludes women. So we change it:

"And everywhere *thy children* be."[1]

What are we doing? Here is a hymn by Isaac Watts, perhaps the greatest hymn writer in the history of Christendom. How dare we change those words? How dare we mess with the integrity of the poetry? My colleague Peter Gomes, at Memorial Church, Harvard, calls it "intellectual vandalism."[2]

No contest—Peter Gomes is right! Others say we are taking the hymn out of historical context, dressing it up to suit our own needs, and that we must live with the scandal of historical limitation—that we are outright revisionists. They are right. Others call it an aesthetic profanity. They are often right. Still others say that by removing the personal pronouns we are turning God into mush. They may be right.

Why, then, do we follow—why do I follow—such an intellectually, aesthetically, historically, culturally erroneous course? Because I believe that for a time, at least, those profoundly important aspects of our communal and personal identity and existence—the aesthetic, the intellectual, and the historical—tend to provide the ground for a social order, sanctioning with divine imagery a distorted, if not denigrating, perception of the humanity of women. Women bear the full image of God no less than do men, and our God includes in her being not simply the power to speak, to create, to challenge the forces of darkness as a male might. Our God also includes in his being the qualities of compassion, care, an eagerness to be connected to the creation and to us, embracing the Godhead, the components we associate with the feminine. As Rosemary Ruether has remarked, and I paraphrase:

> One of the critical principles [of the Christian understanding of God and the meaning of life] is the promotion of the full humanity of women. Whatever denies, diminishes, or distorts the full humanity of women is therefore appraised as not redemptive. From a Christian perspective, whatever diminishes or denies the full humanity of women must be pre- •

sumed not to reflect the Divine or an authentic
relation to the Divine, or to reflect the authentic
nature of things, or to be the message or work of an
authentic redeemer or community of redemption.[3]

If that is true, and I believe it is, then historical,
cultural, aesthetic, and religious concerns and considerations notwithstanding, I for one, with no little trepidation, will take the risk of nudging my formerly sacro-
sanct hero, Isaac Watts, in order that the God he loved
and worshiped may be understood to include the profound gifts of the feminine, in order that women may
be granted full power, full status, full presence, full
humanity in all the orders of creation, from the cosmic arena, to the state, the business world, the church,
the family.

And as for the Bible, I wait with high anticipation
for the new translation of the Revised Standard Version
coming out in the spring of 1990, which uses great care
in its metaphors for God and the human family. It will
not be so dramatically altered as is the translation we
read this morning from *An Inclusive-Language Lectionary.* Nor will it be nearly as male-oriented and patriarchal as the translations in our hymnal. It will be more
accurate, a joy to read, and a challenge to interpret.

We began this morning by asking the questions,
Who are we? Who is God? Our usual answers—the
answers given for generations—are simply not good
enough anymore. Indeed, they do injury and to a great
degree diminish all of us and God. Our God is mindful
of each of us. Male and female, the majestic God em-
braces and sustains us all. Each of us serves as a royal
steward of creation's fullness for the other. Each of us
is made little less than God. Each is crowned with
honor and glory.

8 Advent's Great Scandal

Matthew 11:2-11

Introduction

We said previously, Advent presents a new world breaking in upon us. We proclaim not simply the coming of a newborn babe, we proclaim the entry into our history of "a messianic age." The scandal of Advent, as the accompanying sermon tries to illustrate, lies in a spirituality re-creating the human situation. The world can no longer go on as it has. Jesus shocks religious and civil structures into dramatic and radical change. Advent turns human existence upside down. Jesus fails to stick to religious topics. He has an alteration in the order of things in mind.

This sermon again mentions the old world we find ourselves taking care of, its injustices and conflicts. It tries to help our congregation to see that the steps it may take in changing a system, in alleviating human misery, in taking risks to bring healing, reconciliation, and justice demonstrate the spirituality of Advent and Christmas in a thoroughly faithful fashion.

I am not going to make you wait. I am going to tell you right off the nature of Advent's great scandal. It is the spirituality of Jesus. Advent's great scandal is the spirituality of Jesus! Recall today's passage. John the Baptist lies in prison waiting for something to happen. He had been wandering around the countryside cursing corruption and deceit in high places. He tore into the hypocrisy of the religious types, mocking their smugness, heaping contempt on their complacency. He angrily attacked the political leadership, finally ending up in prison because he called King Herod an adulterer to his face. John, you see, readied himself for a new world. He believed it to be right around the corner. John saw our old world, top-heavy with brutality, fraud, and falsehood, coming to an end. He laid the ax to the root of the tree and expected it to topple momentarily. And the one he knew would inaugurate the new era was the one he had recently baptized in the Jordan: Jesus of Nazareth.

But nothing happened. John looked around for something new in public leadership and social harmony, but nothing! The same old crowd remained in charge. The same dreadful things oppressed his people. What's going on? he wondered. Is Jesus really going to make any difference? Did I place my bets in the wrong place? So John sent some of his own friends to ask Jesus one of the pivotal questions of that or of any age: "Are you the one for whom we wait? Or should we look for another?" You remember how Jesus answered. He did not say, "Yes, I am the one." He did not say, "No! Look somewhere else." Jesus answered John in a peculiarly ambiguous fashion:

> "Go and tell John what you hear and see: the blind receive their sight, the lame walk, the lepers are cleansed, the deaf hear, the dead are raised, and the poor have good news brought to them."

And—and—

> "Blessed is anyone who takes no offense at me."
> —Matthew 11:4–6

Meaning: "Radiant, joyous are those who by my mission are not scandalized."

Scandalized by his mission? What is Jesus talking about? Just this: his coming among us represents a dramatic, 180-degree change in human welfare and social priorities. His coming—contrary to the expectation of political chieftains who seek someone to bless their policies and priorities—Jesus' coming threatens to dismantle their status quos. Jesus' coming, instead of supporting and strengthening current religious practice, turns it upside down and inside out. Religious types consider him finally irreligious, a dangerous radical whose mission subverts their cozy institutions and destroys their chummy ties to the powers that be. Jesus just does not act typically religious. He is out there healing wounds, changing lives, bringing life to the dead, making the maimed whole, giving bad news to society's so-called leaders, and to the marginalized, the down-and-outers, the nobodies, he is offering good news.

Jesus scandalized his time because he just would not fit the definition of spiritual. He spent too much of his time among his country's tougher elements and losers. While people expected professional clergy to dress a certain way, socialize in a particular fashion, talk in modulated and comforting tones, Jesus seemed bent on acting just like everybody else—"a glutton and a drunkard" (Matthew 11:19), they called him—while taking God's case for people most of us would just as soon see out of the way. Jesus was not smooth enough to be a bishop. He was not big on graduate degrees, spent no time in the pulpits of downtown churches, failed to play footsie with mayors, governors, presidents, or business moguls. Jesus did not appear at press conferences or see his name in headlines. When he addressed the courts and civic commissions he refused to use diplomatic language or delicate euphemisms. When he called the religious agencies to their high tasks, he told them it was not the church, synagogue, or temple but rather the world they should worry about: how men and women treat one another, how nations reconcile, how human welfare broadens, how health and wholeness flourish.

We hear nary a word about orders of worship, choir repertoire, church architecture, or church school curriculum; Jesus utters not a sound about stained glass, organ design, or sanctuary decor. Instead, we get a sharp and severe reminder of the promise of re-created human community, a trenchant outline of the prophet's vision, where

the wolf shall live with the lamb,
the leopard shall lie down with the kid.
—Isaiah 11:6

where worship becomes

> to share your bread with the hungry,
> and bring the homeless poor into your house:
> when you see the naked, to cover them,
> and not to hide yourself from your own kin.

—Isaiah 58:7

There it is: a spiritual scandal; no proper asceticism, no pious language, no official credentials, no liturgical apparel, no steady church job, no perks or status—

> "Tell John what you hear and see:
> the lame walk,
> the deaf hear,
> the blind see,
> lepers are cleansed,
> and the poor hear good news.
> And blessed be the one not scandalized
> by the world turned upside down."

—Matthew 11:4–6 (paraphrase)

Question: With Jesus' emphasis on human welfare as the criterion for recognizing his mission and presence among us, how are we doing? How are we doing with human welfare in the world, for instance? I wonder. I think we face what Jesus would call a spiritual crisis right here in our own commonwealth. Economic slowdown, recession, high-tech stagnation notwithstanding, our current state tax conundrum and its impact on the most vulnerable, the least able, the voiceless, the hungry, the sick, those without money, and those who do not vote—as far as we can see, the impact of budget cuts on these people will be devastating. Tax complications, fiscal jargon, economic realities all accepted— from the New Testament's point of view we face not only a revenue shortfall and the crisis of balanced budgets in this commonwealth: we confront a grave ethical dilemma, a profound spiritual issue.

And the issue runs deep and broad. One of our good and sensitive members the other evening passed on a seemingly trivial piece of information. He said one of the groups this church sponsors with money and people power to serve meals to the hungry had served its one hundred thousandth meal. A milestone? Of course it is! And congratulations! But, by heaven, it is a terrible thing too! In the richest country in the world, hunger is an ethical, a spiritual, problem.

Or again, reports are that shelters for the homeless are nearly full to overflowing, and new shelters are probably going to be needed during the coming winter. Our outreach budget puts a drop or so in the leaky shelter bucket set aside to catch such drops. It is necessary; it is appropriate. But something deplorable is happening. The shelter industry is growing. An acceptance of homelessness tends to creep over us. We become anesthetized to and find acceptable increasing homelessness as a reality among us. We prop it up with charity rather than seek justice.

Every time I hear the warm, sentimental tones of some radio announcer on that "all the news all the time" radio station make a plea for a fund for the homeless, I wonder how he can do it without writing an accompanying editorial outraged over the greed and nest-feathering that went on in the Department of Housing and Urban Development over these last ten years. I wonder how we can hear it without a passionate urgency to call on the public officials of these national and state administrations to quit believing housing, hunger, and health to be matters of charity, contingent on how our hearts feel today. I wonder how we can absorb the plea to support another one of the "thousand points of light" without ourselves suspecting something a little askew with a system generating more homeless people and apathetically accepting, if not in truth actively supporting, the priorities of a national administration

whose chief executive officer ends every television address with a "God bless you." What God is he talking
about? The God of the New Testament? Really? For the
New Testament faith, friends, homelessness is not simply an economic problem, not primarily a matter of
national tax policy and treasury reserves. From the
biblical perspective, the economic vacuum indicates a
spiritual vacuum. From the biblical perspective, for all
the econometrics we want to play with, our fiscal deficit
emerges from and is creating a pitiful ethical deficit too.
The building of hunger and homelessness into our political and economic structures and then blatantly encouraging volunteers and charitable giving to pick up the
pieces and to bail out myopic public officials reflects not
only fiscally bankrupt public coffers, but morally bankrupt public policy. Would we put our defense budget up
for charitable giving? Would we entrust public safety to
"a thousand points of light"? Why, then, the budgets
dealing with matters of education, hunger, health, housing, and human welfare? These matters confront us
with the very stuff of Jesus' spirituality.

And what about our church? We face no less a
spiritual crisis here. The other evening our church council wrestled with the budget for next year. We raised
salaries, calculated health benefits, assured ourselves
we could light and heat our sanctuary, sustained the
program, paid the preacher. But we too reflected the
increasingly precarious economic conditions and pathology of the surrounding community: higher costs, dimin-
ishing income. As stacked against the public need, the
relatively puny amounts this church contributes to the
so-called "safety net" dwindled. And we can say, with
everybody else, "That's just the fiscal reality." But let us
not kid ourselves! For those of us who contribute to this
church and those of us who build its budgets we face not
simply fiscal reality; we face a serious spiritual problem.

During these Advent days we see members of the
Salvation Army corps standing on the street corners,

tinkling their bells, blowing their trumpets, trombones, and tubas, pleading for some spare change. The founder of the Salvation Army, General William Booth himself, recognized this practical, irreligious, unchurchy spirituality of Jesus.

> It is no better than a ghastly mockery to call by the name of One, who came to seek and save that which was lost, those churches which, in the midst of lost multitudes, either sleep in apathy or display a fitful interest in [ceremony]. Why all this apparatus of temples, of meeting houses, to save men from perdition in a world which is to come, while never a helping hand is stretched out to save them from the inferno of their present life? Is it not time, that, forgetting for a moment their wrangling about the infinitely little and the infinitely obscure, they should concentrate all their energies on a united effort to break the terrible perpetuity of perdition and to rescue some at least of those for whom they profess their Founder came to die?[1]

Right on, William Booth! God save us from a disastrous confusion over who we are called to be and what we are called to do.

In this Advent season, as we sing our hymns and say our prayers, as we retell the sacred stories, listen to the choir's anthems, and rejoice together in this warm and beautiful room, as we revel in the poetry, re-create the images, and join in singing carols, I pray we never forget the stark and glorious event behind our celebration. It is not sentimental. It is not romantic. It is not nostalgic. We celebrate One who, as the hymn proclaims,

> comes to break oppression,
> To set the captive free,
> To take away transgression,
> And rule in equity.[2]

We celebrate One who answers the question of the ages, "Are you really the one, or are we to look for another?" We celebrate One who answers that question from a spirituality sunk in the very guts of human affairs:

> the blind receive their sight,
> the lame walk,
> the lepers are cleansed,
> the deaf hear,
> the dead are raised,
> and the poor have good news brought to them.
>
> —Matthew 11:4–5

And might this continue: "And radiant are those, yes, joyous, who see my new creation not as offense, not as scandal, but as invitation, as privilege, as blessing."

PART THREE

Political Power

9 A Nation Like Any Other?

1 Samuel 8

Introduction

The presidential election of 1988 included some intense discussion about the place of the American Civil Liberties Union in American life. Vice President George Bush, running as a Republican, accused Massachusetts Governor and Democrat Michael Dukakis of being a "card-carrying member" of the American Civil Liberties Union. The Vice President was, of course, attempting to paint the ACLU as something less than patriotic and to taint it with subversive overtones. By association, the Vice President hoped his opponent would be seen in those questionable tones as well.

Civil liberties are always a debatable issue. As some wise one insisted, "Your liberty stops where my nose begins." That is one way of looking at the debate. But even more, civil liberties are vulnerable to limitations advocated by the powerful. The rights of speech, assembly, and religion included in the Constitution's Bill of Rights come under frequent fire by those, on the one hand, who fear the truth in new ideas, and by those, on the other hand, who are simple demagogues and dance to the current political tune.

The sermon "A Nation Like Any Other?" was delivered the Sunday before the 1988 election. It emerges from reflection on one of the great political polemics found in the Old Testament: Samuel's speech warning Israel against the abuse of power inherent in monarchy. Samuel is terribly worried about civil liberties! The sermon uses, as well, the story of a deacon of the Old South Church in Boston, Samuel Adams, and his crusade for civil liberties in the eighteenth century. It emphasizes again the risks inherent in political hierarchies and concentrations of power. It points to the flaw in human institutions that justifies their own hegemony by deceiving themselves and seeking to persuade others of their own lofty purposes.

This theme makes a difference in the common life of a church. In our case here in Boston, I've always liked to think of the Old South's being home to a variety of public forums dealing with controversial issues emerging from its history with civil liberties. Groups unable to find space elsewhere frequently call on the church to provide a venue so that words of renewal and empowerment may be offered. The church's facilities have been open to agencies like Amnesty International, battling for human rights across the world. Those who struggle to mitigate the problems of refugees or to wipe out the death penalty find a home among us. Civil liberties make a high claim on the agenda of any public church.

Last Sunday, on what was scheduled to be an off day, the Vice President of the United States, George Bush, went to Philadelphia. There this Yankee Episcopalian met with John Cardinal Krol, attended a private mass, and stood with Cardinal Krol for a photo opportunity,[1] essentially receiving the cardinal's blessing. Not to be outdone, the governor of Massachusetts, Michael Dukakis, appeared in a number of churches across the country; with choirs resplendent in the background, surrounded by local clergy and politicians, he offered his message to cheering congregants.[2] Politics and religion, two very powerful forces, were joined in time-honored American fashion again this year.

Now religion and politics make some people uneasy, to be sure. But the marriage of religion and politics resides in the very foundations of the biblical faith. Take that monumental encounter offered by the author of Samuel. It describes a political convention that throws the usual TV-sanitized affair into pale, insipid light. That passage from First Samuel contains ideological confrontation, favorite sons, virulent conflict over tradition and innovation, lofty and uncompromising principles, a tilt toward mob rule. It makes the presidential debates of 1988, by comparison, look positively soothing.

The narrator of First Samuel describes an event signaling an entirely new era in the governance and identity of Israel. For hundreds of years, Israel existed as a theocracy, ruled by charismatic spiritual leaders called judges. But these theocrats hung on to office too long. Power made them complacent and venal. In addition, the populace perceived that international relations were becoming increasingly complex, threatening, and delicate. A new movement, the monarchists, began to agitate and organize for a strong central government. They wanted to be just like other nations. They wanted a king. The narrator describes a dramatic confrontation interweaving religion and politics. He gives us a terrific political convention.

This Old Testament political convention takes place at Ramah. Samuel, the last of the great religious and political leaders, presides. The debate begins. "Give us a king!" demand the monarchists. "We want to be like every other nation." "God is our king!" cry the theocrats. "Our loyalty lies with God's will." The convention breaks into a near riot, and somebody prods the band to play "God Bless Our Israel" until the crowds quiet down.

Polemics become the order of the day. The most spirited, memorable, and eloquent speech comes from the lips of Samuel. There he stands, an old man, seasoned in leadership, semiretired, ashamed of his crooked and lazy sons, ready to defend the grounds of his leadership in this last, glorious stand of the theocrats. And Samuel pours it on. In the tradition of classical, prophetic, populist, campaign oratory he exclaims:

"Our adversaries say they want a king. They want to be like every other nation. Fine and good. But let me tell you what kingship means. A king will build a defense juggernaut that will boggle your minds. He will draft your sons for his wars, he will send them to the trenches and to their deaths to satisfy, not the public good, but his own vanity. A king will confiscate your property for military bases. He will seize your agricultural produce and divert it to his own military and political ends. The king will destroy the domestic economy and plead national security. He will build a monstrous bureaucracy and conscript your children to serve

in it at his discretion. He will claim the right of emi-
nent domain over your property and offer it as bribes to
his cronies. And taxes? 'You ain't seen nothin' yet!' If
you believe he will tax us for the general welfare, forget
it. The king will tax us in order to pay his lackeys,
subsidize his sycophants, support fawning bureaucrats,
and indulge dependents who gorge themselves at the
public trough. Everything we own or earn—our savings
accounts, our estates, our family treasures—will be sub-
ject to his insatiable greed and self-aggrandizement.
You seek security? You'll get slavery. You pursue political stability? You'll get tyranny. You want national
leadership? You'll get oppression. And when finally you
comprehend your self-destructive obsessions, it will be
too late. You will have no voice, no power, no point of
appeal, no rights, no nothing. And, worst of all, your
prayers for redress will return to you void."

Samuel finishes. The convention goes berserk.
Cheers, boos, placards, marches, bands, ecstasy, gavels,
more "God Bless Our Israel." Then comes the roll call.
It is not even close. The monarchists win. Samuel and
the theocrats take a humiliating licking. Samuel ac-
cedes to the will of the majority and promises to deliver
a king. Everyone goes home, and Saul lies just around
the corner. The new age begins.

So the joining of religion and politics is nothing new.
When political candidates show up in church and Prot-
estants embrace cardinals; when they end all their
partisan, self-serving convention speeches looking you
straight in the face and murmuring, "God bless you"—
they continue a tradition not wholly unknown to the
biblical faith.

But the tie between religion and politics can be
found not only in the scripture, it can be found as well
right here in Massachusetts, and even closer to home,
in Massachusetts Congregationalism. And closest to
home, right here in the Old South Church in Boston. I
have been intrigued, for instance, by inclusion of the

American Civil Liberties Union in this year's political debate. Vice President Bush treats the ACLU with contempt and derision. Governor Dukakis tries to dissociate himself from it. Sad! But again, really, what else is new under the sun? Civil liberties are always vulnerable to contempt and ridicule by those who hold power. Isn't that what the prophet Samuel warned his own people about? "Get yourself a king," he said, "and he'll arrogate all rights unto himself." Samuel is onto something.

But there is another Samuel, whose legacy in defense of civil liberties we cherish in this church. He served as deacon here. You will find a plaque in his memory on that back wall. The plaque reads:

> Samuel Adams
> A member of this church
> Born September 16, 1722
> Died October 1, 1805
> To give his story at full length
> Would be to give a history of the
> American Revolution

When people visit this church, some say they come because of its "historic interest." Indeed, you will often hear this church described as "historic Old South Church." Why? Partly because the deacons of this church, the members of this church, the leadership of this church, became, in effect, an "American Civil Liberties Union" one hundred fifty years before the current ACLU came into existence. Indeed, you have heard me say on other occasions that Richard Hale, the former historian of the commonwealth of Massachusetts, used to define the American Revolution as a struggle between the king's Parliament and the deacons of Old South Church. What was at stake? What did this church stand for? Why is Adams' plaque on our rear wall?

One of the great tensions of every polity is the tension between power and liberty. The great debates preceding the American Revolution dealt with the disposition of power. John Adams, our Calvinist ancestor, continued to search for the right definition of power, finally arriving at the word "dominion." To our New England ancestors, like Adams, writes Bernard Bailyn, "power meant the dominion of some men over others, the human control of human life: ultimately force, compulsion."[3] Political hierarchies with a lone sovereign at the top commanding, demanding, exercising autocratic power, represented the political style of the time. Discussion around power, he continues, "centered on its essential characteristic of aggressiveness: its endlessly propulsive tendency to expand itself beyond legitimate boundaries." Our forebears saw power's tendency as "trespassing," "encroaching," "grasping," "tenacious in its nature," "relentless in its will to seizure."[4]

And what did power encroach upon? What did it seize, invade, trespass? What was aggressive power's "natural prey, its necessary victim"? Liberty, law, and right. "Alas!" wrote one observer, "power encroaches daily upon liberty with a success too evident, and the balance between them is almost lost."[5]

And this insight about power's aggressive tendency rooted itself in another conviction: the real culprit in power's incessant encroachment on human and civil liberties lay not so much in the character of power, but in the character of human beings. Human nature contained the susceptibility to corruption and the lust for self-aggrandizement. "Such is the depravity of mankind," declared Samuel Adams, speaking for the Boston town meeting, "that ambition and lust of power above the law are predominant passions in the breasts of most men." Adams continues: Human instincts in citizens of "all nations combined the worst passions of the human heart and the worst projects of the human mind against the liberties of mankind."[6] Neither reason nor religion, Adams believed, could provide effective constraints against the reach and lust for power inherent in human nature.

Understanding this tendency of the human heart and human institutions to seek control, Samuel Adams—agitator, propagandist, theoretician—went to work, first of all, to limit the power of the king and Parliament to infringe on the rights of English citizens who happened to live in the colonies. And, secondly, failing in those efforts to negotiate the limits of the king, Adams pursued independence from the Crown and began with others to design a new polity in which liberty and power were balanced. In 1777 Adams wrote to his wife,

> I am not more convinced of anything, than that it is my duty to oppose to the utmost of my ability the designs of those who would enslave my country; and with God's assistance I am resolved to oppose them till their designs are defeated or I am called to quit the stage of life.[7]

What was the result of Adams' civil liberties crusade? "In Europe," Madison wrote, "charters of liberty have been granted by power. America has set the example . . . of charters of powers granted by liberty."[8] The constraints of power are determined by the rights of human beings, rather than the rights of human beings determined by the wielders of power.

Doesn't this conviction lie at the heart of our republic today? I think so. The very genius of our polity lies in the conviction that the majority rules. Nonetheless, even "as great a blessing as [democratic] government is," writes the Reverend Peter Whitney,

> like other blessings, it may become a scourge, a curse and a severe punishment for the people. What made it so, what turned power into a malignant force, was not its own nature so much as the nature of man—his susceptibility to corruption and his lust for self-aggrandizement.[9]

The skepticism of Samuel Adams and his generation concerning human nature and its impact on the exercise of power is no less a risk with a supposedly republican polity than it is with an autocracy. No President, no Vice President, no governor, police chief, or general, no Congress nor any court can finally be trusted to protect the liberties of citizens. We, the people, independent of the organs of government, are finally the ones responsible for our own liberty. As Learned Hand wrote, "Liberty lies in the hearts of men and women; when it dies there, no constitution, no law, no court can do much to help it."[10]

It is that legacy of independent responsibility for liberty that Deacon Samuel Adams left us. As Pauline Maier informs us, Adams wrote in a letter to Richard Henry Lee in 1785, "I firmly believe that the Benevolent Creator designed the republican form of government for man."[11] But even within republics, Adams fully understood the revolutionary, threatening, dangerous, yet absolutely necessary implications of staking out the protection of liberty. He understood the relentless attack the agents of liberty would incur from the status quo. Contempt, derision, subversion of human rights and civil liberties and those who uphold them by the powers that be, sadly enough, tend to be the usual course in our fallen world. Even so, Adams believed that republics offered liberty and peace the best chance. Yearning for the experiment of the new colonies on the North American shore to be tried all across the world, he speculated to Richard Henry Lee, "Will the lion ever associate with the lamb or the leopard with the kid 'till our favorite principles shall be universally established?"[12]

A paragraph from Pauline Maier's revealing book *The Old Revolutionaries: Political Lives in the Age of Samuel Adams* catches the essence of our theme. The paragraph ties together in an ingenious fashion the prophet Samuel, and his fierce polemic in behalf of civil liberties, with our deacon Samuel and his profound and courageous pursuit of civil liberties. To Samuel Adams, writes Maier, revolutionary republicanism constituted only a revival of the ways of his New England ancestors. "The Continental Congressmen [meeting unpretentiously in York, Pennsylvania, following the British capture of Philadelphia in 1777] reminded Adams of those early New Englanders who were satisfied with bread and cheese, or 'clams and mussels.'" It was, Adams claimed, "the principles and manners of New England" which produced "the spirit which finally has established the independence of America." And the "genuine principles of New England," he suggested, were quite simply "republican principles."[13]

> Thus, Adams, in what had been for his ancestors a New Israel in this New World, took on the role of his Old Testament namesake, Samuel the prophet, insignificant except as God's instrument, who chastised Saul for his perfidy, knew that kingship was a rejection of the Lord's rule and wicked in His eyes, and remained determined that for all their falling from grace, his people's wanderings through the wilderness would not become "a fool's errand but the foundation of a new state conformable to God's will."[14]

How about it: are we a nation like any other? As the prophet Samuel warned, will those who slander the protectors of civil liberties carry the day? Or can we confound the prophet Samuel and sustain our deacon Samuel in the divine struggle to protect, as he said, those "principles and manners of New England" which produced "the spirit which finally has established the independence of America"?

10 When Presidents Talk of God

Jeremiah 2

Introduction

Presidential rhetoric is replete with God-talk. Few U.S. Presidents come before the nation without invoking "the Almighty" in one way or another. Addresses before Congress, presidential inaugurals, and party nominating conventions offer massive forums for reminding the citizenry of the Divine partiality toward this nation, its polity, its standing in the world. And, of course, we are subtly—nay, blatantly—reminded of the President's discernment of and personal accord with the Divine wishes.

In addition to these public political occasions, any number of Presidents attend special prayer breakfasts and welcome representatives of religious communities to the White House. In most cases, through "photo opportunities," the effort appears to be the pursuit of religious sanction for the personal piety and public policy of the President. It is seldom good religion. It is frequently good politics. Abraham Lincoln was not only a shrewd and subtle politician, he was also a first-class biblical theologian. He did not resist God-talk any more than his predecessors or his successors. But his God-talk resisted implying an intimate connection or commitment of the Divine favor to the policies of the Republican Party, the Union armies, or a favored national destiny. Lincoln's God seemed to be one with impartial compassion upon our human lot. To Lincoln, no one could make a special claim on God's mercy and judgment, though he was convinced that mercy and judgment were exercised amid the ambiguity and tragedy of human existence. Lincoln seemed to understand the transcendence of God and, obversely, the almost blasphemous traps of identifying too closely one's political and social hopes with the Divine plan.

Because our modern Presidents have immersed themselves in God language, because Divine partiality riddles United States identity, encouraging a sense of self-righteousness and special privilege, the following sermon was written as a benchmark for presidential God-talk. It was delivered on Lincoln's birthday. As we enter the nineties with severe issues before us, I pray we in

the churches may bring to the public realm Lincoln's tragic
sense of the human condition and his faith in a transcendent
Providence bearing us through the worst we may do to one
another.

In the last two weeks President Ronald Reagan has
delivered three major addresses, to the United States
Congress, to the Religious Broadcasters of America, and
to the citizens of his Illinois hometown and his alma
mater, and in each of them God has played a major
role. Reagan, as he said to Congress, quoting Carl
Sandburg—"saw America in the crimson light of the
rising sun, fresh from the burning, creative hand of
God."[1] President Reagan referred to a God he wants
acknowledged formally in the public school classrooms
of the United States: a God clearly against something
called "big government," a God who feels the same way
about abortion as about slavery, a God allied with a
people, says the president, "who were never meant to be
second best, and who never will be."[2] And to the broadcasters, the president affirmed that "no matter where
we live we have a promise that can make all the
difference—a promise from Jesus to soothe our sorrows,
heal our hearts and drive away our fears." The president said the latter in a hotel dining room with TV
cameras focused on him while campaigning again for
the presidency of the United States. Reporting it, the
New York Times called it a "Sermon on the Stump."[3]
    The eagerness to identify this nation and one's office
with God is as old as this country. In 1630, John
Cotton, as if initiating a new exodus, preached to John
Winthrop's fleet as it left England for these shores: "I
will appoint a place for my people Israel, and I will
plant them, that they may dwell in a place of their own,
and move no more [II Sam. 7:10, KJV]." Cotton affirmed "the divine right to occupy the land."[4] Ever since
those Puritans founded this commonwealth, we have
been, as G. K. Chesterton remarked, "a nation with the

soul of a church."[5] "In America," said another, "the country was the religion."[6]

Our Presidents reflect this religiosity—this national messianism. We find their state papers drenched with divine references. Woodrow Wilson faced a new age with feelings "sweeping across [his] heartstrings . . . like some air out of God's own presence."[7] Warren G. Harding affirmed a belief in "the God-given destiny of our Republic."[8] John Kennedy assumed the national task of protecting the "rights of man" because they come "not from the generosity of the state but from the hand of God." Kennedy urged

> With a good conscience our only sure reward, with history the final judge of our deeds, let us go forth to lead the land we love, asking His blessing and His help, but knowing that here on earth God's work must truly be our own.[9]

Ronald Reagan's references to God emerge from a long and, profoundly rooted heritage beginning right here in Massachusetts, which John Winthrop himself dreamed would be a "Modelle of Christian Charity."[10]

Thus, our question: When Presidents talk of God, what god are they talking about? I am going to use as our primary reference for presidential God-talk the President whose one hundred seventy-fifth birthday we celebrate today. Abraham Lincoln, as Sidney Mead writes, "is the spiritual center of American history."[11] Reinhold Niebuhr considered Lincoln "the most original of all American religious thinkers,"[12] and Harvard's Dean Willard Sperry called Lincoln "one of the few men in history, our own history and all history, whose religion was great enough to bridge the gulfs between the sects, and to encompass us all."[13] All American political God-talk can be measured for integrity by looking to Abraham Lincoln.

In the first place, Lincoln provides us with a glimpse of a transcendent, sovereign God whose freedom will not be compromised by the whims, the wills, the objectives of finite human beings. This God of Abraham Lincoln works organically in our history: ruling nations mysteriously, unpredictably; working among us toward a final historical redemption unfettered by what we believe that redemption should look like and what its timetable should be. Providence, we call it: all things—crises, tragedies, even civil conflict—working for good, for those who love God; yet in this incomplete and unfinished world, seen as through a glass, darkly.

Lincoln expresses this faith in many places. To Eliza Gurney, a well-known Quaker woman who visited him in 1862 and prayed he be given light and wisdom from on high to see through the dilemmas of the war, Lincoln responds by telling her he has sought God's aid in assisting him to discern God's purposes amid this great, indeed "fiery" trial. He continues:

> But if after endeavoring to do my best in the light which he affords me, I find my efforts fail, I must believe that for some purpose unknown to me, God wills it otherwise. If I had had my way, this war would never have commenced; if I had been allowed my way, this war would have ended before this, but we find it still continues; and we must believe that he permits it for some wise purpose of his own, mysterious and unknown to us; and though with our limited understandings we may not be able to comprehend it, yet we cannot but believe that he who made the world still governs it.[14]

Lincoln's God: a sovereign Providence standing over against—indeed, apart from—us, yet working among us for just and peaceful ends; a God whose will we may seek, perhaps discern, even join, but never control. Lincoln has his ground there.

Second, Lincoln possesses a prophetic sense of God's being in contention with the nation. He stands with

Jeremiah, Isaiah, Amos, Micah, in understanding the convulsion of the Civil War as a judgment on a nation that built into its very foundations the enslavement of the black race. This was no glorious war, as Julia Ward Howe would have it in the "Battle Hymn of the Republic." This war resulted from the horrendous sins of the nation's founders, countenanced for two and one-half centuries, saturating and corrupting the whole communal fabric. "The parents have eaten sour grapes, and the children's teeth are set on edge" (Ezek. 18:2).

And so with Lincoln. Calling for a national day of fasting in April 1863, a few months after the Emancipation Proclamation, Lincoln expresses this conviction of a nation at war because of its betrayal of a God whose righteousness is sovereign. He insists, first of all, that nations, as well as individuals, are called to confess their sins and transgressions. Then he continues:

> And insomuch as we know that, by God's divine law, nations, like individuals, are subjected to punishments and chastisements in this world, may we not justly fear that the awful calamity of civil war, which so desolates the land, may be but a punishment inflicted upon us for our presumptuous sins to the needful end of our reformation as a whole people?[15]

Then Lincoln crystallizes this specter of divine judgment in one of the most striking passages of his Second Inaugural Address:

> Fondly do we hope, fervently do we pray, that this mighty scourge of war may speedily pass away. Yet if God wills that it continue until all the wealth piled by the bondsman's two hundred fifty years of unrequited toil shall be sunk, and every drop of blood drawn with the lash shall be paid for by another drawn with the sword, as was said three thousand years ago, so still it must be said, "The judgments of the Lord are true and righteous altogether."[16]

One wonders, nearly one hundred twenty years after this profound observation: are we yet paying for the two hundred fifty years of "unrequited toil," for every "drop of blood drawn with the lash"? Here we see Lincoln's faith—a sovereign and just God whose purpose will not be mocked in human history, whose judgments on us and on our nations remain true and righteous altogether.

This faith of Abraham Lincoln's in a sovereign God transcending all of us, holding all individuals and nations accountable, including Lincoln himself, enabled Lincoln to avoid the temptation snaring most every political leader, president, and moralist in American history: the temptation to identify the working of Providence with one's own cause or ambition, one's own party, platform, policy, and national goals. As Reinhold Niebuhr writes,

> Alone among statesmen of the ancient and modern periods, Lincoln had a sense of historical meaning so high as to cast doubt on the intentions for both sides, to put the enemy in the same category of ambiguity as the nation to which his own life was committed.[17]

Again, in the Second Inaugural, Lincoln puts that civil conflict in a dramatically moral arena.

> Neither party expected for the war, the magnitude or the duration which it has now attained. Neither anticipated that the cause of the conflict might cease with, or even before, the conflict itself should cease. Each looked for an easier triumph, and a result less fundamental and astounding. Both read the same Bible and pray to the same God; and each invokes His aid against the other.[18]

There then follows a passage of such depth and insight, it can be found in virtually no other statesperson's moral perspective. In it, Lincoln relates the moral judgments we must make in the midst of our history to the reservations we must hold about those moral commitments, just because we live in history unfinished, broken, biased, and self-interested. First of all, Lincoln makes the moral judgment, a judgment he fought for: "It may seem strange that any man should dare to ask a just God's assistance in wringing their bread from the sweat of other men's faces."[19] With that strong moral judgment about slavery, he then offers the reservation, "But let us judge not that we be not judged. The prayers of both could not be answered—that of neither has been answered fully."[20]

Do you see what Lincoln does? He disengages the ultimate purposes of Providence from what he knows to be his own partial and self-interested moral judgments. Lincoln refuses to identify *his* understanding of the meaning of the Civil War—in this case, national survival and a democratic polity for white and black—with what in faith he believes to be the ultimate purposes of Almighty God. Lincoln will not say God is on our side. He prays only that, stumbling and struggling through human life, trying to discern the signs of the times, he might perchance tilt from time to time toward God's side. Talk about presidential humility!

And the converse of this humility? What can it be but magnanimity? Lincoln planned to treat the states of the Confederacy as if they had never left. That conviction makes its way again into the haunting passages of the Second Inaugural:

> With malice toward none, with charity for all; with firmness in the right as God gives us to see the right, let us strive to finish the work we are in, to bind up the nation's wounds; to care for him who shall have borne the battle, and for his widow, and his orphan—and do all as may achieve and cherish a just and lasting peace among ourselves and with all nations.[21]

Most every other president fashions God into a national or tribal deity, a cheerleader for his own policies and prejudices. Not so Lincoln. No other American president publicly identifies himself, his policies, or the national destiny as Lincoln does: partial, flawed, immersed in the moral binds and dead ends of the human dilemma, worthy not so much of a sentimental blessing as of divine contention, and of being called into question—of stringent judgment by a sovereign and righteous God. No other president, thus understanding his own precarious position before God, identifies so completely with the wounds of an apparent enemy. No other president so transcends his immediate circumstances as to render so poignantly the tragedies, the paradox, the ambiguities of our human condition: "Let us judge not that we be not judged." Is it any wonder James Russell Lowell saw in Lincoln

> a hero new,
> Wise, steadfast, in the strength of God, and true.
> How beautiful to see
> Once more a shepherd of mankind indeed. . . . [22]

In February 1861, on his way to Washington and the first inauguration, Lincoln stopped in Trenton, New Jersey. While speaking to the legislature, he recalled his favorite boyhood book, Weems's *Life of Washington*. He remembered especially the hardships entailed in crossing the Delaware at Trenton, and went on to say:

> I recollect thinking then, there must have been something more those men struggled for; something more than even national independence; something that held out a great promise to all the people of the world to all time to come; I am exceedingly anxious that this Union, the Constitution, and the liberties of all the people shall be perpetuated in accordance with the original idea for which that struggle was made, and I shall be most happy, indeed, if I shall be

an humble instrument in the hands of the Almighty,
and of this, his almost chosen people, for perpetuat-
ing the object of that great struggle.[23]

"An humble instrument in the hands of the Almighty"—isn't this the most any of us dares pray for?
As we witness those in power so often succumbing to
the delusion of their being the Almighty's *righteous*
instruments, we had best be wary. And yes, we need to
regain Lincoln's agony, his tragic sense, his humility
as we surrender ourselves to a sovereign, just, and
mighty God.

11 Can the Church Take a Stance at Election Time?

Revelation 13:1-8

Introduction

The citizens of the United States face two separate but interlocked political and religious issues. The first issue we call "church and state." It centers on the relationship of religious institutions to social policy. A second issue, sometimes confused with the first, we call "religion and politics." This issue focuses on the extension of personal convictions to the quality of life in the public realm. Both issues create heated discussion, debate, and conflict. In both cases, antagonists use two profound authorities against each other: the Bible and the United States Constitution.

Massachusetts, of course, was one of the last theocracies of the Western world. In 1833 Massachusetts' support of an established church finally collapsed. But the religious and ethical controversies continue. Christians of many denominations and inclinations continue to pursue legislative action to extend their social ideas across the commonwealth.

In 1986, the voters of Massachusetts were faced with two such controversial opportunities. The November ballot included two amendments to the state constitution. They were known as "Question 1" and "Question 2." The first dealt with constitutional ramifications of a woman's choice over carrying a pregnancy to term. The second eased constitutional restraints on public subsidies for independent schools.

Question 1 was summarized as follows:

> The proposed constitutional amendment would allow the legislature to prohibit or regulate abortions to the extent permitted by the United States Constitution. It would also provide that the state constitution does not require public or private funding of abortions, or the provision of services or facilities for performing abortions, beyond what is required by the United States Constitution. The provisions of this

amendment would not apply to abortions required to prevent the death of the mother.

A YES vote would change the state constitution to allow the state legislature to regulate or prohibit abortion or the funding of abortion, to the extent permitted by the United States Constitution.

A NO vote would leave the state constitution unchanged and continue state constitutional protection of abortion.[1]

Question 2 was summarized as follows:

The proposed constitutional amendment would allow the expenditure of public funds for private schools and private school students.

It would remove primary and secondary schools from the list of non-public institutions barred from receiving public aid and would allow public money, property or loans of credit to be used for founding, maintaining or aiding those schools. The proposed amendment would also allow public financial aid, materials, or services to be provided to a non-public school student requesting such aid, but only if that school does not discriminate in its entrance requirements on the basis of race, color, national origin, religious belief, sex or physical handicap. The state legislature would have the power to impose limits on aid, materials, or services provided to students.

A YES vote would change the state constitution to allow government aid to non-public school students, to the extent allowed by the United States Constitution.

A NO vote would keep in the state constitution the current restrictions on government aid to non-public schools and non-public school students.[2]

Although the following sermon deals with these two specific problems in the Massachusetts context, I believe it conveys a mood and tone as well as particular convictions that might be appropriate for a pastor to make at election time. Both the understanding of the particular issue of abortion, but perhaps even more so, the understanding of church and state might be helpful for pastors facing the complex mix of issues coming during the nineties.

In Massachusetts the issues of "reproductive freedom" continue to stir intense debate and political activity. The issue of church and state will always be with us. I cannot make any claims for the impact of the sermon, here. Both Question 1 and Question 2 were defeated. I think preachers bear responsibility for tackling these issues.

On Tuesday, most of us go to the polls again. We will face a motley collection of candidates promising personal integrity, improved public services, lower taxes. Good luck to them. We will also be asked to vote on a number of questions, emerging in a remarkable and truly wonderful way from our citizen-based polity, questions whose impact will make a significant difference in our public life. They deal with issues such as choice in wearing an automobile seat belt and timetables for cleaning up toxic waste. There are, however, two questions, numbers 1 and 2, in which churches, synagogues, and other private and public agencies find themselves deeply engaged. Question 1 deals with the range of choice women have in electing, for any number of reasons, an abortion. Question 2 deals with the matter of public subsidies for private and parochial schools. These two propositions touch, it seems to me, two bedrock convictions that churches in our tradition hold very dear. The first of these convictions centers on "church and state." The second of these convictions focuses on "religion and politics." The line between these two matters is not always clear, but I want to do some thinking about them with you this morning.

We will address this matter of "church and state" first. Public funding for private schools is a matter of "church and state." The Massachusetts Constitution currently forbids the use of public money for any "charitable or religious undertaking," including religion-sponsored "primary or secondary schools." Question 2 seeks to extend new forms of aid, material, and services to nonpublic schools through the state treasury and local budgets. If passed, it will have a decidedly negative impact on revenues available for public education, and it will alter significantly the state-church balance.

The tendency toward separation of public from private religious institutions is a peculiarly American phenomenon. From time to time one hears that we can attribute our understanding of church-state separation to the Reformation. I wish that were altogether true. Unfortunately, Reformation churches were no more immune to bucking for state prerogatives and national establishment than any other supposedly God-ordained body. Indeed, one of the ironies of U.S. history lies right here in Massachusetts.

The founders of this commonwealth, who came here partly to practice freely their religious convictions, declared illegal the religious practice of those they considered unorthodox. Our Puritan ancestors banned the spiritualist Anne Hutchinson. They hanged the Quaker Mary Dyer on Boston Common. They sent the Baptist Roger Williams packing off to Rhode Island. They even possessed the audacity to consider the Old South Church in Boston the *Third* Church in Boston, when, indeed, the First Baptist Church had been founded some five years before ours. The Old South is really the "Fourth Church" in Boston. But, you see, in seventeenth-century Massachusetts, Baptists did not count. In addition, while most of the colonies followed Virginia in abolishing state churches and providing for religious freedom, this commonwealth, through its constitution of 1780, empowered local authorities to tax citizens in support of the parish church. Now, most towns and parishes in Massachusetts contained a vast majority of Congregationalists. As a result, Jews, Catholics, Anglicans, atheists, agnostics, and endemically resistant Baptists found themselves subsidizing Congregational clergy and maintaining their buildings. They hated it! And rightly so. This went on for over half a century.

Finally, three years after a court case decided by a Unitarian chief justice subjugated us Congregationalists to second-class religious status, along with the Jews, Catholics, Anglicans, and Baptists—three years after we found ourselves compelled to cough up subsidies for the upkeep of so-called Unitarian heretics—on election day, November 11, 1833, by a referendum margin of ten to one, "religion was disengaged as an engine of the state."³ This holy commonwealth was the last to end establishment of religion.

In truth, the genius of the American understanding of the church-state separation does not come from the Reformation. It does owe a lot to the Baptists, thanks to Roger Williams, and to the tenacious, brilliant Isaac Backus, who fought the Massachusetts establishment tooth and nail. But really, this peculiar, ingenious, original national polity emerged out of the Enlightenment. And, as much as I regret to say it, not from Massachusetts, but from Virginia. Sick to death of the coercion of mind and heart demanded by establishment religion, James Madison and Thomas Jefferson succeeded in forging the Virginia Statute of Religious Liberty. Over the fury and fire of the established Anglican Church, the General Assembly of Virginia proclaimed that no one

> shall be compelled to frequent or support any religious worship, place of ministry whatsoever, nor shall be enforced, restrained, molested, or burdened in his body of goods, nor shall otherwise suffer on account of his religious opinions or belief; but all [people] shall be free to profess, and by argument to maintain, their opinion in matters of religion, and that the same shall in no wise diminish, enlarge, or affect their civil capacities.⁴

Madison remarked that in Virginia, "the ambitious hope of making laws for the human mind has been forever extinguished."⁵ Jefferson called it the "severest contest"⁶ of his life. To this day, the tradition of religious institutions, free from the oversight, control, and management of the magistrate by the church, stands at the heart of our common life. To be sure, the resultant freedom of worship, belief, and creed leads to a wild anarchy of denominations; each free, through the "benign neutrality" of the state and its own means of persuasion, to pursue its chosen goals.

But every religious group is guaranteed the opportunity to articulate and practice its faith without special powers or favors for one or for all. Each is free to establish its own institutions and educational enterprises, to persuade people to attend them, to raise money for them, to propagate what they want within them, with equal lack of access to the public treasury. No religious group can, by law, gain preferential benefits from the public coffers at the expense of all others. Thanks to Madison and Jefferson, this is how we have succeeded in maintaining social harmony and public fairness in a religiously pluralistic society.

Separation of church and state is a principle and a reality profoundly worth hanging on to and protecting. It would be, I believe, threatened if Question 2 were passed on Tuesday. Speaking this morning, not for you, but to you, as a legatee of those nineteenth-century Congregationalists who were arrogantly complacent and deservedly humiliated, as a lover, in this case, not so much of Cotton Mather, but of Thomas Jefferson, I will vote "No" on Question 2.

But separation of church and state does not mean separation of religion from politics. Our religious convictions can be extended to the public realm through political action and the ballot box. Now, right here, churches face grave difficulties. Congregations are organized for reasons other than our political convictions. Nonetheless, we do include men and women of strong political inclinations, frequently contradicting one another. And the more strongly held the conviction, the more nearly a religious certainty it becomes. And more— when we Christians relate our religion to politics, we tend to become overwhelmingly self-righteous. Many of us equate our religious and political commitments. As Reinhold Niebuhr wrote:

> We regard every political decision as simply derived from our faith. All [of us] are naturally inclined to obscure the morally ambiguous elements of [our]

political cause by investing it with religious sanctity. . . . The tendency to equate our political with our Christian convictions causes politics to generate idolatry.[7]

Hard political decisions need to be made, but we need make them with humility and magnanimity, realizing that different people, with equal sincerity and wisdom, arrive at contrary conclusions. We need to remember that none of us makes a complex political decision from a purely rational, purely moral, purely Christian stance.

Now why these moral yellow flags? Because I believe Question 1, dealing with the matter of a woman's choice in the matter of abortion, offers an illustration of the possibilities and dangers of mixing religion and politics. Question 1 is an amendment to the Massachusetts Constitution, giving the Massachusetts legislature full powers to "regulate or prohibit abortions" within the bounds of the U.S. Constitution, as interpreted by the U.S. Supreme Court. It also insists that "no provision of the Massachusetts Constitution shall require public or private funding of abortion, or the provision of facilities therefore, beyond that required by the U.S. Constitution."[8]

Why is this a matter of religion and politics? Simply because we deal here with the most profound matters of life and death, of personal choices, of equal access by poor people to the quality medical care afforded the rich. We wrestle in this abortion matter with what it means to be a human being, and how the dogma and conscience of one religious camp interface with those of another. We encounter the question of who will be granted authority to decide the most private, intensely ambivalent, and frequently tragic decision a woman faces about her life: her life's meaning, the meaning of those lives she brings into the world, the nature of her family, and the ties she has with so many others. Religion deals with these questions of meaning, choice, community, life, death, and tragedy. Politics does too.

In the matter of abortion the Roman Catholic Church, as a matter of doctrine based on natural law, an understanding of what constitutes our full humanity, and standing on time-honored grounds, considers abortion to be murder. Its followers are not the only ones. I suspect a number of you within this congregation, for very powerful and deeply held moral, humane—indeed, religious—reasons, believe the same thing. In general, the so-called evangelical wing of Protestantism is against any choice in the matter. In a passionate effort to be consistent, they campaign against both abortion and the death penalty. If you feel this way, if after analysis of the issues at stake you perceive abortion to be murder, then you had better try to put a stop to it, lock, stock, and barrel. Question 1 offers you that opportunity. You can vote to severely curtail abortions. You can vote "Yes." Your ballot will be an extension of your religion. But please, if you vote "Yes," do so with a sense of contrition and humility, and with a view to all the lives at stake.

Others of us in this congregation will vote "No" on Question 1, and our ballots may be no less an extension of our religious convictions. We will take our stance with the Massachusetts Council of Churches, understanding that in a pluralistic society public money is inevitably used for some things that offend our consciences. We will weigh the options and, grasping the hard choices many teenagers and women have to make, we will try to make possible the excellence in medical facilities for everyone. We will vote "No," believing the state legislature to be the last place these ethical and family issues should be decided. Indeed, following the lead of the Massachusetts Council of Churches, some here believe that:

Abortion is an agonizing moral dilemma for many Americans. In weighing conflicting values, many conscientious Christians, no less life-affirming than others, recognize the value of human potential in fetal life, but give heavy moral preference to the value of the feeling and thinking of women and families. The moral problem of abortion, morever, cannot be resolved by simple, indiscriminate prohibitions, since the rightness or wrongness of the act depends upon the peculiar circumstances of each case. Government in complex societies cannot make or enforce legal generalizations to cover justly the multitude of uniquely personal dilemmas of modern women.

In this setting, many Christians are convinced that the best policy on abortion is the continued recognition of a constitutional right for all women to make personal decisions in light of their individualized situations, and in response to the moral counsels of their religious traditions. This policy will not avert the moral dilemma of abortion in America. But it will avoid discrimination against persons in religious traditions which deny that abortion is an absolute evil. And it will prevent re-enactment of the countless tragedies for women and men in the now-romanticized era before abortion was legal in the United States.

For us, the compassionate focus in this political campaign should be on the question of how to help women prevent undesired pregnancies, rather than prohibiting tragic choices in the aftermath of the private—and public—failures.[9]

However you vote on Question 1, do it with fear and trembling.

Church and state, religion and politics. Can the church take a stand at election time? Yes? No? Perhaps? Friends, go to the polls on Tuesday. Cast your ballots. And whatever choice you make, God be with you.

12 Just How Radical a Commitment?

John 13:21-30

Introduction

During Lent, 1983, the sermons dealt with decisive encounters Jesus had with other Gospel characters and, finally, with Paul. On Palm Sunday, the spotlight shone on Jesus and Judas. The question lying behind the sermon is, "Why did Judas betray Jesus?" As one broods about it and reflects on the commentaries, conventional wisdom points toward Jesus' refusal to join in Judas' political zealotry as the answer. Judas ostensibly joined "the Twelve" because he envisioned a cadre of political revolutionaries bent on throwing out the Roman colonialists and setting up a revolutionary state. But Judas discovered, after three years of mucking around the Galilean countryside, that Jesus' realm was "not of this world." Thus, disillusioned, cynical, and himself feeling betrayed by the failure of what he perceived to be Jesus' promise, Judas turned Jesus over to the authorities for some paltry pieces of silver.

We can understand that. After all, we want to follow those who will take care of the enemy. But what if the enemy is us? That is the gist of the following sermon. Jesus is not only out to change those whom Judas recognizes as political problems, he is out to change Judas and his crowd too—and that is just too much for Judas. This insight, by the way, is powerfully conveyed in a little book by James Smart entitled *The Quiet Revolution.*[1]

And your attention needs be called to something else. The references in the sermon to "the painted bays" and the "beautiful room" embrace the then current refurbishment of Old South's sanctuary. As our church moves into the nineties, the challenges of a deepening New England recession and war and rumors of war confront us. We will encounter some increasingly difficult issues. And I suspect many other churches will too. We will find the challenges of bricks and mortar, the questions of survival and mission, putting us severely to the test. We will discover "just how radical a commitment" as we assemble our

127

budgets, allocate our resources, and arrange our priorities. At this writing, in the winter of early 1991, we have some tough questions to answer.

Judas! A name dripping with opprobrium and tangled with the worst things we do to one another. Judas: he used a kiss of peace to "do in" the most gracious and compassionate life we have ever known. When we choose the names of our children, we look to the friends and family of Jesus: Mary, Peter, John, James, Elizabeth. But Judas? Never! We use the name only as a metaphor for those involved in the shabbiest human circumstances.

How shall we explain Judas? Nikos Kazantzakis suggests that Jesus chose Judas to betray him because he believed Judas to be the strongest of the disciples, and therefore most able to bear the contempt of history. Some observers speculate that Judas hatched a plot to force Jesus into violent encounter and ultimate victory over the Roman colonialists, but the plot failed; Jesus would not play along. A few others suggest a greedy cynic who might sell his mother for thirty pieces of silver.

Now, each of these theories seems plausible, and we might like to give credence to one or all of them. Each one of them, however, gets us off the hook. Judas as superhuman hero, divine foil, or satanic scoundrel can be dismissed as a human aberration: "He's not like me." But I do not think Judas is an aberration. He may be all too true to human life, and not the kind of human life exemplified by Attila the Hun or the Boston Strangler. Judas is true to life as you and I face it on a day-to-day basis, life with all its ambiguities, its conflicting loyalties, its shifting values. It could be that Judas threw himself more completely than the other disciples into what he perceived to be Jesus' ministry. It could be that Judas finally saw more clearly than any other disciple the full dimensions of that ministry. Let us look at him.

First of all, we can never forget that Jesus chose Judas. Jesus recognized in Judas a person willing to move with him into the future. Remember that rich, young ruler who went away sorrowfully when Jesus presented to him the terms of discipleship? Not so Judas. He accepted Jesus' terms. He left his occupation. He gave up his address. He chose poverty. He committed himself to Jesus' ministry for the long term.

In addition, we need to remember that Judas shared the mission of Jesus. Jesus not only chose him, Jesus sent him out. Judas went into the world with his colleagues, two by two. Jesus commissioned Judas no less than the others with the ministry of preaching, teaching, healing, and human restoration. The Evangelists give no indication of Judas subverting the gospel, compromising it, misunderstanding it, or misinterpreting it. Indeed, it is the disciples most confused about the gospel—Peter, James, and John—after whom we name our children.

One more fact: Judas kept the disciples' purse. Now, I do not know about the organizations you belong to, but the ones I belong to elect treasurers who are honest, prudent, and of impeccable character: no shifty eyes, no quick hands, no spendthrifts. Treasurers are persons whose competence in money matters elicits trust. We see in Judas no basically evil man. The novels, the plays, the cinema, the great works of art, they may have Judas wrong.

What, then, leads Judas to betray Jesus? Most commentators say that as a Zealot, a profoundly committed Jewish nationalist who wants to rid his land and people of Roman imperialism, Judas betrays Jesus because Jesus disillusions him and refuses to mount the military campaign against the Roman occupation that any self-respecting Jewish Messiah would organize. In

short, Jesus fails to lead a national liberation movement; Judas becomes disenchanted and sells him out.

But I wonder. Could it be that Judas' betrayal
emerges not so much from disappointment as from
terror; not so much from disillusionment as from panic?
Look at it this way. Suppose Judas does harbor revolutionary political objectives. Those objectives are born of
his profound loyalties to an independent Jewish nation
and to the hopes and promises of Judaism itself. Judas
wants the Romans out. Judas wants his own people in
charge at any cost. Judas may well be disillusioned
when Jesus refuses to pursue those violent and revolutionary ends. I suspect Judas' disillusionment would
compel him to pack his bags and search for an armed
guerrilla band, prepared to take Pilate's palace by force.
But he does not do that. He betrays Jesus to the Jewish
and Roman authorities instead. Why? Could it be because Jesus represents a threat not simply to Roman
imperialism, but also to Jewish nationalism? Could it
be because Judas sees that Jesus will change not only
the Roman governor, Pilate, and all he stands for, but
also Judas and all he stands for?

Judas is ready for the overthrow of the Romans, but
I think Jesus threatens more than that: he takes on
Judas too. Jesus condemns as hypocritical and self-
defeating the national and religious foundations sustaining Judas. Jesus calls some of Judas' religious he-
roes "[children] of hell" (Matt. 23:15). Jesus is going to
take on his own people, a people needing not only
release from the tyranny of Rome but release from the
tyranny of their own self-satisfied nationalism and religious complacency. For Judas the true patriot, the true
believer, that assault is too much. Jesus turns out to be
far more radical than Judas, the self-proclaimed revolutionary, anticipates.

Judas is a disciple who places limits on his commitments to Jesus. After accepting the call to discipleship,
Judas discovers what he cannot give up. After confess-

ing surrender to Jesus, Judas finds some bastions he wants to keep for himself. Jesus represents a new age, and Judas wants to hang on to the old. Jesus talks about a universal human community, Judas wants to protect his turf, his particularity. Judas wants to build barriers around himself, his nation, his church, his class, his neighborhood, his gender. Jesus wants to dissolve the power inequities of imperialism, to be sure. But he reminds Judas to be wary of his own temptation to exercise force and drape it in God's will. So long as Jesus lays off, Judas is happy. So long as Judas believes Jesus may lead a crusade against national and religious enemies, Judas hangs on. But the radical questioning by Jesus of everything Judas holds dear? Judas is not ready for that!

Are we? This coming Holy Week brings to a crisis the promise and challenge of Jesus Christ for all of us. The extent of Jesus' commitment—death, on a cross, for love's sake—throws light on our own commitment. In the deepest impulses of our national life, for instance, there remain challenging, difficult, and costly tasks ahead. Did you know that today marks the anniversary of President Lincoln's death? When we recall his dreams and his vision of a nation indivisible, we can, like Judas following Jesus, lay claim to his dreams. Then we discover that the reaching of the dream is not just a task for someone else. The Emancipation Proclamation, the Second Inaugural Address, the Fourteenth Amendment bear ethical consequences for all of us. They command changes in housing patterns, in hiring, in zoning, in schooling. In their vision of a just and peaceful human community they pose threats to the way we have been doing things that may shelter our traditions and our prejudices. "The dogmas of the quiet past are inadequate to the stormy present. . . . The occasion is piled high with difficulty and we must rise with the occasion. As our case is new, so we must think anew and act anew."[2] Lincoln said that. In a sense it

is what Jesus said to Judas—and it proved too much
for him.

Or again, Christ throws light on the scope of our
commitment as a church, on my commitment as your
brother in Christ. Every time I contemplate the refurbishment of our sanctuary, and the portents of beauty
for this room, my adrenaline runs. And I say to myself,
"What a glorious room this will be to celebrate the
mystery and majesty of God! What a marvelous room in
which to sing about and to tell the stories of Jesus!
What an inspiration this splendid room will be to the
human spirit!" And yet? And yet, I hear the resounding
cadences of Matthew 25 in a suffering, unjust, and
economically skewed world:

> "I was hungry and you gave me food, I was thirsty
> and you gave me something to drink, . . . I was
> naked and you gave me clothing, I was sick and you
> took care of me, I was in prison and you visited me."
>
> —Matthew 25:35–36

And I hear Bishop Desmond Tutu, under house
arrest in South Africa, suffering under and standing up
against apartheid, saying to Christians everywhere:

> God is on the side of the oppressed, the poor, the
> despised ones. We must say these things even if they
> make us suffer. . . . This is the essence of Christian-
> ity, because Jesus said, "Unless you take up your
> cross and follow me, you cannot be my disciple." An
> affluent, comfortable church cannot be the Church
> of Christ—an affluent church which uses its wealth
> for itself.[3]

Do you see now why Judas could not bear with
Jesus? It was not because Jesus disillusioned him. It
was because Jesus made him uncomfortable. It was
because Jesus took the things Judas took for granted,

the assumptions he lived with, and turned them upside down, challenging him to be a new person, a new human being, fit for a new age.

As we move into this Holy Week, we encounter again the dimension of our own commitment. Who can assess that commitment but God and ourselves? I know not where you stand. As for me, I find Jesus posing tough questions about my ultimate loyalties. I find myself confronted by that haunting Holy Week question:

Were you there when they crucified my Lord?
Were you there when they crucified my Lord?
Oh! Sometimes it causes me to tremble,
tremble, tremble.[4]

Amen.

Postscript

I suppose the question might be asked, "So, did your efforts to encourage a public vocation for Christian ethics amount to anything? Did you discover men and women among your congregation 'worthy to raise issues'?" I suspect, as in all human endeavors of this nature, the answer is at best mixed.

First of all, as suggested in the Introduction, I stand in a long line of creative pastors and congregations. My immediate predecessor, Frederick Meek, possessed of a first-class intellect and a broad capacity to synthesize religious convictions and public issues, provided me with a springboard. I was in no way bringing to the Old South congregation anything novel. Frederick Meek's profound concern for the quality of life in the city, his sensitivity to international issues, his despair about the Vietnam War all touched on in his eloquent sermonic discourses, provided an ethos where my material, if not exactly agreed with, constituted the normal fare for the morning. I was blessed with a congregation already "worthy to raise issues" and sensitive to its publicly ethical vocation.

The approach one takes to issues, however, makes a profound difference in how a congregation responds. Recently in a nearby town a very able, highly intelligent pastor was driven from his church by his congregation. He was a visible fellow; his stands on public issues were, to say the least, controversial, tilting strongly to the Left. I believe his congregation would not only have tolerated his stances but listened to his case, indeed, they knew what they were getting when they hired him. But, somehow, his certainty that his way coincided with Christ's began to get in the way of his ministry. His congregation was not so much over- whelmed by the issues he laid before them. They were finally overwhelmed by his impatience, curtness, and the condemnatory tone he brought to discussions.

This risk of righteousness presents itself to all of us in the ministry who wish to deal with public issues and ethics. There we stand, "ten feet above the congrega- tion" in our pulpits, slashing away at a captive audi- ence. Our people, I believe, are sympathetic to us. They want to listen. They want to hear a word of grace as well as a mandate for life. We frequently lose our audience, not because of the issues we tackle, but through the tone we use. I'll never forget a wonderful man in Old South I lost, unfairly, I believe, because I mistook cynicism for humor. I say unfairly because, although he might have disagreed with me on some issue and might finally decide he must leave, he did leave because of a cynical and cutting remark I made about a certain public official. The public official had been corrupt, mean, and vengeful. He was prosecuted, sent to prison, "found Jesus" there, and became, in short order, an exemplary citizen. I couldn't believe it and said so. Well, I was wrong, and not only about the public official—I was wrong to attack his motives for a laugh.

This matter of touching issues fairly is crucial. Fin- ger pointing without sympathy for the human condi- tion, scolding a congregation without including oneself in the problem at hand, derisive laughter and put-down of any of God's children flies in the face of the gospel (you shall love your enemies, that is, will their good as you will your own good). The heart of the gospel pro- claims no one lives outside of God's love, no one is beyond the boundary of God's redemptive, transforming power, on the one hand. On the other, the gospel shows us all to be sinners, vulnerable, fragile, myopic, self-interested, self-deceived. Issues are complex, affecting different people in different ways: ideologically, economically, personally. Dealing fairly, compassionately, and with an open heart toward those who disagree sustains a parish ministry. People will listen—they may even change their minds—if they know they may disagree and not be considered beyond the pale or read out of the Christian assembly.

Of course, some people take exception because they heartily disagree with a particular stance or stances. I still retain a letter from a parishioner who made, among other things, a most cordial, eloquent, and infuriated case against the use of "inclusive language" in the Doxology. In addition, as a member of the Armed Forces Reserve, he sensed a personal attack when I made reference to defense budgets. But one of his comments was especially telling: he said that because of a combination of factors I tended to speak in "abstractions"—in "theories"—and this was disconcerting and an impediment to intimate conversation.

Touché. Indeed, my correspondent touched two very troublesome points for clergy. The first has to do with abstraction. This tradition of the "learned ministry," the heritage of the academy and the church, the background of scholarship and ideas included in the credentials of the Reformed clergyperson, can create a chasm between us and our flocks. My parishioner added that I was also an "authority figure," so, for him, anyway, this abstract arguing of mine left him in what he perceived to be a diminished position personally and intellectually. What a shame! This tendency to abstraction is the occupational hazard of clergy types. It can be an escape from engagement with reality. It can be simply intellectual laziness, an esoteric shortcut to avoid the nuances and mess of the human predicament. I suspect fear and pride lead us to it. Obfuscation can cover a ton of ignorance. And, after all, now that we have our divinity degrees, there ought to be some special "lingua franca"—some commonly understood highbrow terms of expression—for us.

But the real problem he laid open resides in our distancing ourselves from our people. I suspect they wonder, Do you really know what it's like to be me? Do you know what the real world is like? Do you believe life in the street is as good as it may be here in church, or that what we find in the workplace reaches the heights of ethical purity you rumble on about? Do you think our choices are as clear as you put them? Do you recognize the ambiguities of our lives, the ambivalence behind most of the decisions we make, the fact that one person's defense budget overkill is another's livelihood?

I will never forget a colleague's relating the story of a friend who asked him if God was as good as Jesus. It is a question coming from the tooth-and-claw world of most of our parishioners. They wonder if we know it, understand it, share their agony as they try to survive within it. They wonder if we can offer any grace for their accommodation to it. Can we? Can I? It's the test of authenticity in our personal relations and in our preaching.

Now and again, of course, we have our little victories. On the front page of the *Boston Globe*, Easter Sunday, 1990, there appeared an article about the baby boom generation making its way back into our churches.[1] The writer quoted the sociologists, the psychologists, the social pathologists, the ministers, and representatives of the generation itself about this sneaking back into church. One of the interviewees joined the Old South Church on Palm Sunday, 1990. "Why did you join?" asked the journalist. The new member did not answer, "Because I liked the music [or the preaching, or the fellowship, or the education]." She answered, "Because I thought the outreach the church was doing was important." Feeding the hungry, clothing the naked,

doing the public ministry drew her to our community. I
believe that answer tells truth at the very heart of the
gospel. With all the other gimmicks we provide these
days for our consumer-oriented church shoppers, one
wonders if we are not hardened atheists, failing to trust
the power of the Word and the persuasive authenticity
of service.

My fondest hope, of course, lies in the possibility
that preaching had something to do with the strength
of the outreach ministries attracting the young woman.
The aforementioned cumulative impact of "Social Gospel" preaching, I hope, tends to nourish and encourage
the church's outreach. Not long ago, another young
woman and her husband were among those who joined
Old South. As usual, in a preliminary meeting, we went
around the circle introducing ourselves to one another.
Why did these people choose to join Old South? we
wondered. Well, of course there were many reasons: the
music, the space, the people, the program, the friend-
ships, the opportunities for service. But this particular
couple suggested they had been church-hopping and
found in Old South an emphasis in Word and worship,
mission and outreach that seemed to them all of a
piece. Of course, that unity does not occur all the time.
The Word and worship, mission and outreach no doubt,
to some, feel like an enormous dichotomy. I may fail to
connect the two dimensions of ministry. The congregation may fail to connect the two. But over a period of
time, I trust, Word and worship, mission and outreach
become for the people of our congregation the unified
dynamic of our congregational life.

Some sermons, of course, touch people just at the
right time in their pilgrimage. The sentence prayer
delivered at the beginning of the sermon, trusting the
Holy Spirit to make of our words the Word, may well be
answered more frequently than any of us dare guess.
One woman, formerly wrestling with a variety of midlife
adjustments, now invested in one of the significant

poverty ministries in Boston, found in one sermon what she described as "joy and mission going hand in hand." "I've been pondering recently the essential binding of faith with obedience," she wrote. "The latter is not a popular concept in this narcissistic era." Later, she hung a cross around her neck, not simply as a piece of jewelry, but as a sign of the nature of her readiness for obedience in a tough social-justice ministry. That our mumbling and stammering can serve as a nudge tilting a person's life one way or another for good illustrates again the transforming power of the Holy Spirit.

Surely the AIDS crisis confronts us all in a unique and terrible way. A sermon entitled "The Gospel Confronts Us with a Claim Over Life and Death" seemed to let loose a great reservoir of pain, terror, and grief. One woman wrote to say just the naming of the de-mons tormenting her life—homosexuality, homophobia, AIDS; "taboos," she said—relieved her. She informed me of her own lesbianism and now participates in the church's Gay and Lesbian Fellowship. Another person remarked she "thought a great deal about AIDS" and discussed it with her premedical students at a regional university. "It's hard not to be depressed in the face of the statistics," she wrote. "But you reminded us of the healing work of the church. And the church is each one of us." That particular sermon apparently continues to provide encouragement and support to a number of men and women seeking safe harbor in a troubled and threatening world. It provides a way of entry for our congregation's thinking about and acting amid this relentless plague.

The matter of public policy and the homeless in Boston has received its share of pulpit concern over the last few years. The church has involved itself in signifi-cant efforts to alleviate the problem. It has established, for at least three years, a housing office to help discover and implement a strategy for churches in relation to the housing crunch. The church has invested a quarter

of a million dollars in a community housing and investment fund. It has cosigned notes with community
organizations in order to facilitate loans. It has sup-
ported a part-time researcher on a city councilman's
staff to draft legislation encouraging a process known
as "link deposit banking." This process monitors the
commitment of local banks to community investment. It
promises those banks with high marks in local community investment the lion's share of deposits from a
variety of the city's coffers. In addition, the church has
sponsored symposia focusing on state and federal legislation and resources for housing. It has encouraged its
members to support legislators who take the housing
crisis seriously.

Question: Has the addressing of this problem from
the pulpit of the church made any difference? Other
than expressing the sympathy of the minister for approaches to tackling the issue, has preaching really
made any impact? It is hard to measure, of course. One
man, deeply involved in the "shelter industry," insisted the church not only provide assistance for the
shelters on an emergency basis. He pled for church
support of public policy measures on the basis that
charity would not solve the problem. The mechanisms
of the public sector needed to be engaged as well. In his
plea he cited sermonic references to the differences
between charity and justice. Another person, respond-
ing to a sermon describing the perverse housing policies
of the Reagan Administration, and herself working to
alleviate the problem on an emergency basis, joined our
housing committee and wrote me saying she believed
almost all other issues should be set aside until this
terrible blight was resolved. Again and again, with a
gentle passion, she eagerly lobbies our outreach and
housing committees to work for systemic change. And,
bless her heart, she'll bring a homiletical quote along to
buttress her case.

Yet I make no great claims for specific sermons'

triggering specific actions. When an impact is made, it seems to be "in the fullness of time": someone brooding about an issue and the preacher somehow articulating—providentially?—what the listener may have believed all the time.

And can we see any difference in the public realm? Now and again. A renovated house for previously homeless people makes its way into the city's housing stock. But it is a drop in the bucket. The legislation dealing with "link deposit banking" is making its way through the city council and then the state legislature. Some AIDS victims are cared for, some local community organizations begin to get their hands on the levers of power, and we can rejoice in this. And yet? And yet, no matter how we might be eager to enter the "public vocation of Christian ethics," as one looks for ethical change for the better in the public realm the results appear to be relatively slim. For all our preaching, our enormous contributions to charity, our efforts to put both "rescuers" and "transformers" on the line, the quality of life in the city and world does not seem to improve very much. As James Reston used to say, our technological progress seems to outrun our ethical sensitivities. I recall George W. Webber of the East Harlem Protestant Parish surveying changes in East Harlem as a consequence of the Parish's work there. He calculated differences here and there, but concluded the neighborhood suffered no less from drugs, poverty, housing, education, and medical catastrophe than when the EHPP started in 1948. Why such inertia? For me, Reinhold Niebuhr puts his finger on the hazards of high expectations for our preaching and teaching a public vocation for Christian ethics in a fallen world. In a sermon entitled "The Wise Men and the Mighty Men," Niebuhr writes:

> The wise and learned men, the seers and saints, the philosophers, social scientists and religious idealists who seek to dissuade the oligarchs of our era from

their suicidal policies conform to a very old tradition. Since the dawn of history there have been men of wisdom and virtue who stood before the king to speak the truth. . . . Their advice and wisdom seemed to them so logical and persuasive that they never could understand why the potentates should not be convinced of evil by their strictures and turned to paths of righteousness by their guidance. The priest or the philosopher standing before the king is a perpetually recurring picture in human history. It is symbolic of the contest between the conscience of society and its imperial impulses, a contest in which the conscience does not frequently gain the victory.[2]

Why not? Because, in short,

the men of conscience do not understand the tragic facts of human nature. They do not know to what degree the impulses of life are able to defy the canons of reason and the dictates of conscience.[3]

This insight reminds us again of our true predicament. It reminds us that all the good works of preaching, teaching, healing, and striving for God's dominion are finally partial, limited, fraught with the bent of self-interest, immersed in class and cultural perceptions, dealing with forces and principalities of our own making, and frustrated by our incapability to unmake or salve the consequences. Realizing our impotence and self-deception, we are thrown back again to the inevitability of the cross in our kind of world. From that point we live in the sure and certain hope that nothing we do in church or out of it can finally bring the new creation among us. Our only hope is the searching, probing, re-creative grace of the compassionate, world-transforming God at work through our Sovereign and Savior, Jesus Christ.

Notes

Introduction

1. *The Public Vocation of Christian Ethics*, ed. Beverly W. Harrison, Robert L. Stivers, Ronald H. Stone (New York: Pilgrim Press, 1986).

2. Reinhold Niebuhr, "Morality and Politics," in *Essays in Applied Christianity*, ed. D. B. Robertson (New York: Meridian Books, A Living Age Book, 1959), 90.

3. Ibid., 92.

4. Reinhold Niebuhr, "The Christian Witness in a Secular Age," in *Christianity and Power Politics* (New York: Charles Scribner's Sons, 1952), 210–11.

5. Ibid., 211.

6. Reinhold Niebuhr, *The Children of Light and the Children of Darkness* (New York: Charles Scribner's Sons, 1944), xi, xii.

7. David Buttrick, "Some General Hermeneutical Proposals," *Homiletic: Moves and Structures* (Philadelphia: Fortress Press, 1988), 277.

8. Dieter T. Hessel, *Social Ministry* (Philadelphia: Westminster Press, 1982).

9. Ibid., 27–28.

10. Ibid.

11. Richard Neuhaus, *The Naked Public Square* (Grand Rapids, Mich.: Wm. B. Eerdmans Publishing Co., 1984).

12. Max Stackhouse, *Public Theology and Political Economy* (Grand Rapids, Mich.: William B. Eerdmans & Co. for the Commission on Stewardship of the National Council of the Churches of Christ in the U.S.A., 1987), 2.

13. Ibid.

14. Hamilton Hill, *History of the Old South Church*, vol. 2 (Boston: Houghton Mifflin Co., 1890), 548.

15. George A. Gordon, *The Eternal Pledge of Progress* (Cambridge, Mass.: Riverside Press, 1899), 2.

16. Reinhold Niebuhr, "The Christian Witness in the Social and National Order," in *Christian Realism and Political Problems* (New York: Charles Scribner's Sons, 1953), 105.

17. Ibid., 106.

18. *Annual Record* (Boston: Old South Church, 1940–41), 31–32.

19. Ibid., 50–51.

20. Frederick M. Meek, "A Perspective on Twenty Years in Copley Square," sermon preached at the Old South Church in Boston on October 30, 1966 (Boston: Old South Church, 1966).

21. Niebuhr, "The Christian Witness in a Secular Age," 216.

Chapter 1

1. Ernest T. Campbell, in *The Riverside Preachers*, ed. Paul H. Sherry (New York: Pilgrim Press, 1978), 127.

2. Ibid., 130.

Chapter 2

1. Woody Allen, "Selections from the Allen Notebooks," in *Without Feathers* (New York: Warner Books, 1975), 9–10.

2. Charles Lukey, in William F. Buckley, "Death of a Christian," excerpt from "Execution Eve and Other Contemporary Ballads," *Reader's Digest* 109 (September 1976): 31–32.

3. Ibid.

4. Daniel Berrigan, quoted in Jim Wallis, *Agenda for Biblical People* (New York: Harper & Row, 1976), 26.

5. Desmond Tutu, *Crying in the Wilderness* (Grand Rapids, Mich.: Wm. B. Eerdmans Publishing Co., 1982), 36.

Chapter 3

1. Woody Allen, "Selections from the Allen Notebooks," in *Without Feathers* (New York: Warner Books, 1975), 8.

2. Ibid.

3. Low Income Housing Information Service, *Federal Spending*

for Housing 1976–1990 (Washington, D.C.: Government Printing Office, 1989), 6.

4. City of Boston Emergency Shelter Commission, *Homeless Census Statistics; October 1983 and February 1988* (Boston, 1988).

5. Ellen S. Bassuk, M.D., et al., "Characteristics of Sheltered Homeless Families," *American Journal of Public Health* 75 (September 1986): 1097–1100.

6. Erma Bombeck, *The Grass Is Always Greener Over the Septic Tank* (New York: McGraw-Hill Book Co., 1976), 157.

7. *Man of the Century: A Churchill Cavalcade*, ed. Editors of Reader's Digest (Boston: Little, Brown & Co., 1965), 123.

8. Harry Stein, *Ethics and Other Liabilities* (New York: St. Martin's Press, 1982), 86.

9. Alan Paton, *For You Departed* (New York: Charles Scribner's Sons, 1965), 23–24.

10. Martin Luther King Jr., "Our God Is Able," in *Strength to Love* (Philadelphia: Fortress Press, 1981), 113–14.

Chapter 4

1. George Adam Smith, *The Book of the Twelve Prophets*, rev. ed. (New York: Harper & Brothers, 1928), vol. 2, 51.

2. Ibid., 52–53.

3. Ibid.

4. Arthur M. Schlesinger Jr., *Robert Kennedy and His Times* (Boston: Houghton Mifflin Co., 1978), 746.

Chapter 5

1. Ann Weems, *Family Faith Stories* (Philadelphia: Westminster Press, 1985), 132.

2. Simone Weil, *Waiting for God* (New York: Harper & Brothers, Harper Colophon Books, 1951), 49.

3. Michel Quoist, "Lord, Why Did You Tell Me to Love?" in *Prayers*, trans. Agnes M. Forsyth and Ann Marie de Commaille (Kansas City, Mo.: Sheed & Ward, 1963), 117. Used by permission of the publisher.

Chapter 6

1. Elisabeth Schüssler Fiorenza, *In Memory of Her* (New York: Crossroad Pub. Co., 1984), 68–154.

2. Ibid., 124.

3. Christine R. Robinson, *Planning: AIDS* (Boston: United Way of Massachusetts Bay, 1987), 16.

4. Arthur Kleinman, M.D., *The Illness Narratives: Suffering, Healing and Human Condition* (New York: Basic Books, 1988), 162–63.

5. William Sloane Coffin, quoted in Rt. Rev. John R. Krumm, *AIDS and God's Love* (Cincinnati: Forward Movement Publications, 1987), 2.

6. Ellen Goodman, "For Doctors an AIDS Dilemma That Is Spreading with the Disease," the *Boston Globe*, 25 February 1988, 21.

7. Richard Goldstein, "AIDS and the Social Contract," the *Village Voice*, 29 December 1987, 17.

8. Kittredge Cherry and James Mitulski, "We Are the Church with AIDS," the *Christian Century*, 27 January 1988, 85–88.

Chapter 7

1. Isaac Watts, "I Sing the Mighty Power of God," *Inclusive Language Hymns* (Amherst, Mass.: First Congregational Church, 1984), no. 68. Italics added.

2. Peter Gomes, in conversation.

3. Paraphrased from Rosemary Radford Ruether, "Topics in Feminist Theology," in *Sexism and God-Talk: Toward a Feminist Theology* (Boston: Beacon Press, 1983), 18–19.

Chapter 8

1. William Booth, quoted in Harry Emerson Fosdick, "Service and Christianity," in *The Meaning of Service* (Garden City, N.Y.: Garden City Books, 1920), reprinted in Harry Emerson Fosdick, *The Three Meanings* (Garden City, N.Y.: Garden City Books, 1950), sec. I-c, 14.

2. James Montgomery, "Hail to the Lord's Anointed," *Pilgrim Hymnal* (New York: Pilgrim Press, 1958), no. 105.

Chapter 9

1. Maureen Dowd, "Bush Fights Back on Issue of Elitism," *New York Times,* 31 October 1988, sec. B, 4.

2. Campaign Notebook, "In the Middle of It, Filled with Wonder," *New York Times,* 24 October 1988, sec. B, 5–6; and Associated Press, "Homeless Urged to Vote," ibid.

3. Bernard Bailyn, *The Ideological Origins of the American Revolution* (Cambridge, Mass.: Belknap Press, 1980), 55–56.

4. Ibid., 56.

5. Cato, quoted by William Hicks, "Cato's Letters: No. 73," in *The Nature and Extent of Parliamentary Power Considered* (Philadelphia, 1768; John Harvard Library Pamphlet 24), in Bailyn, 58.

6. Samuel Adams, quoted in Bailyn, 60.

7. Pauline Maier, *The Old Revolutionaries: Political Lives in the Age of Samuel Adams* (New York: Albert A. Knopf, 1980), 43.

8. James Madison, quoted in Bailyn, 55.

9. Peter Whitney, "The Transgressions of a Land" (Boston, 1774), 21–22, in Bailyn, 59.

10. Learned Hand, *The Spirit of Liberty,* ed. Irving Dillard (New York: Alfred A. Knopf, 1960), 190.

11. Maier, 44.

12. Ibid.

13. Ibid., 45.

14. Ibid.

Chapter 10

1. Ronald Reagan, in "Transcript of Message by President on State of the Union," *New York Times,* 26 January 1984, sec. B, 8.

2. Francis X. Clines, "Reagan Turns 73 at Home in Illinois, Saying Nation's 'Self Doubt' Is Over," *New York Times,* 7 February 1984, sec. B, 5.

3. "Sermon on the Stump: An Editorial," *New York Times,* 3 February 1984, sec. A, 28.

4. John Cotton, "The Divine Right to Occupy the Land," in *1493–1754: Discovering a New World,* vol. 1 of *Annals of America,* ed. Mortimer Adler (Chicago: Encyclopaedia Britannica, 1976), 107.

5. Sidney Mead, *The Nation with the Soul of a Church* (Macon, Ga.: Mercer University Press, 1985), 48.

6. Michael Novak, *Choosing Our King* (New York: Macmillan Publishing Co., 1974), 105.

7. Charles Henderson, *The Nixon Theology* (New York: Harper & Row, 1972), 16.

8. Ibid.

9. John F. Kennedy, "Inaugural Address," *1961–1968: The Burdens of Power,* vol. 18, *Annals of America,* Adler, ed., 5–7.

10. John Winthrop, "A Model of Christian Charity," in vol. 1, *Annals of America,* Adler, ed., 109.

11. Sidney E. Mead, *The Lively Experiment* (New York: Harper & Row, 1963), 73.

12. Elton Trueblood, *Abraham Lincoln: Theologian of Anguish* (New York: Harper & Row, 1973), vii.

13. Ibid.

14. Abraham Lincoln, "Reply to Eliza P. Gurney," in vol. 5, *1861–1862, Collected Works of Abraham Lincoln,* ed. Roy Basler (New Brunswick, N.J.: Rutgers University Press, 1953), 478.

15. Abraham Lincoln, "Proclamation Appointing a National Fast Day," in vol. 6, *1862–1863, Collected Works of Abraham Lincoln,* Basler, ed. 155–156.

16. Abraham Lincoln, "Second Inaugural Address," in vol. 8, *1864–1865, Collected Works of Abraham Lincoln,* Basler, ed., 333.

17. Reinhold Niebuhr, "The Religion of Abraham Lincoln," *Christian Century,* 10 February 1965, 173.

18. Ibid.

19. Ibid.

20. Ibid.

21. Ibid.

22. James Russell Lowell, "Ode Recited at the Harvard Commemoration, July 21, 1865," in *The Complete Poetical Works of James Russell Lowell* (Boston: Houghton Mifflin Co., 1897), sec. VI, 344.

23. Abraham Lincoln, "Address to the New Jersey Senate at Trenton, N.J.," in vol. 4, *1860–1861, Collected Works of Abraham Lincoln,* Basler, ed., 235–36.

Chapter 11

1. Office of the Secretary of State, "Regulating or Prohibiting Abortion," in *Massachusetts Information for Voters: The Ballot Questions in 1988* (Boston: 1988), 2.

2. Office of the Secretary of State, "Government Aid to Non-Public Schools and Students" (Boston: 1988), 3.

3. Leonard Levy, *The Establishment Clause: Religion and the First Amendment* (New York: Macmillan Publishing Co., 1986), 38.

4. Edwin S. Gaustad, ed., *A Documentary History of Religion in America to the Civil War* (Grand Rapids, Mich.: Wm. B. Eerdmans Publishing Co., 1982), 261.

5. Dumas Malone, *Jefferson and His Time,* vol. 1, *Jefferson the Virginian* (Boston: Little, Brown & Co., 1948), 279.

6. Ibid., 274.

7. Reinhold Niebuhr, "Christian Faith and Political Controversy," in *Love and Justice: Selections from the Shorter Writings of Reinhold Niebuhr,* ed. D. B. Robertson (Philadelphia: Westminster Press, 1957), 59.

8. Office of the Secretary of State, "Regulating or Prohibiting Abortion," 2.

9. Massachusetts Council of Churches, *Abortion Amendment: Reproduction Question #1: No!* (Boston: 1986).

Chapter 12

1. James D. Smart, *The Quiet Revolution* (Philadelphia: Westminster Press, 1969), 97–108.

2. Abraham Lincoln, "Annual Message to Congress, December 1, 1862," in vol. 5, *1861–1862, Collected Works of Abraham Lincoln,* Basler, ed., 537.

3. Desmond Tutu, *Crying in the Wilderness* (Grand Rapids, Mich.: Wm. B. Eerdmans Publishing Co., 1982), 32–33.

4. African American spiritual.

Postscript

1. Richard Higgins, "Religion Reviving for Baby Boomers," the *Boston Globe*, 15 April 1990, sec 1, 1.

2. Reinhold Niebuhr, "The Wise Men and the Mighty Men," in *Reflections on the End of an Era* (New York; London: Charles Scribner's Sons, 1936), 39–40.

3. Ibid., 48.

Works Cited

Allen, Woody. *Without Feathers.* New York: Warner Books, 1975.

Bailyn, Bernard. *The Ideological Origins of the American Revolution.* Cambridge, Mass.: Harvard University Press, 1960. Reprint, Cambridge, Mass.: Belknap Press, 1980.

Bassuk, Ellen S., M.D., L. Rubin, and A. S. Lauriat. "Characteristics of Sheltered Homeless Families." *American Journal of Public Health* 76 (September 1986): 1097–1101.

Boesak, Allan. "Jesus Christ the Life of the World." In *If This Is Treason I Am Guilty.* Grand Rapids, Mich.: Wm. B. Eerdmans Publishing Co., 1987.

Bombeck, Erma. *The Grass Is Always Greener Over the Septic Tank.* New York: McGraw Hill Book Co., 1976.

Boston Globe. 25 February 1988; 15 April 1990.

Buckley, William F. "Death of a Christian." Excerpt from "Execution Eve and Other Contemporary Ballads." *Reader's Digest* 109 (September 1976): 31–32.

Buttrick, David. *Homiletic: Moves and Structures.* Philadelphia: Fortress Press paperback, 1988.

Cherry, Kittredge, and James Mitulski. "We Are the Church with AIDS." *Christian Century,* 27 January 1988, 85–88.

City of Boston Emergency Shelter Commission. *Homeless Census Statistics: October 1983 and February 1988.*

Cotton, John. "The Divine Right to Occupy the Land." In *1493–1754: Discovering a New World.* Vol. 1 of *Annals of America,* edited by Mortimer Adler. Chicago: Encyclopaedia Britannica, 1976.

Fiorenza, Elisabeth Schüssler. *In Memory of Her.* New York: Crossroad Pub. Co., 1984.

Fosdick, Harry Emerson. "Service and Christianity." In *The Meaning of Service*. Garden City, N.Y.: Garden City Books, 1920. Reprinted as a book in *The Three Meanings*. Garden City, N.Y.: Garden City Books, 1950.

Gaustad, Edwin S., ed. *A Documentary History of Religion in America to the Civil War*. Grand Rapids, Mich.: Wm. B. Eerdmans Publishing Co., 1982.

Gordon, George A. *The Eternal Pledge of Progress*. Cambridge, Mass.: Riverside Press, 1899.

Hand, Learned. *The Spirit of Liberty*, edited by Irving Dillard. New York: Alfred A. Knopf, 1960.

Harrison, Beverly W., Robert L. Stivers, and Ronald H. Stone, eds. *The Public Vocation of Christian Ethics*. New York: Pilgrim Press, 1986.

Henderson, Charles. *The Nixon Theology*. New York: Harper & Row, 1972.

Hessel, Dieter. *Social Ministry*. Philadelphia: Westminster Press, 1982.

Hicks, William. "Cato's Letters: No. 73," In *The Nature and Extent of Parliamentary Power Considered*. Philadelphia, 1768; John Harvard Library Pamphlet 24. Quoted in Bernard Bailyn. *The Ideological Origins of the American Revolution*. Cambridge, Mass.: Belknap Press, 1980.

Hill, Hamilton. *History of the Old South Church*. Vol. 2. Boston: Houghton Mifflin Co., 1890.

Inclusive Language Hymns. Amherst, Mass.: First Congregational Church, 1984.

An Inclusive-Language Lectionary: Readings for Year C. Atlanta, New York, and Philadelphia: Cooperative Publication Association: John Knox Press; Pilgrim Press; Westminster Press, 1985.

Kazantzakis, Nikos. *The Last Temptation of Christ*. Translated by Peter A. Bien. 1960. Reprint. New York: Simon & Schuster, A Touchstone Book, 1967.

Kennedy, John F. "Inaugural Address." In *1961–1968: The Burdens of Power*. Vol. 18 of *Annals of America*, edited by Mortimer Adler. Chicago: Encyclopaedia Britannica, 1976.

King, Martin Luther, Jr. *A Testament of Hope: The Essential Writings of Martin Luther King Jr.* Edited by James M. Washington. San Francisco: Harper & Row, 1986.

————. *Strength to Love.* Philadelphia: Fortress Press, 1981.

Kleinman, Arthur, M.D. *The Illness Narratives: Suffering, Healing and Human Condition.* New York: Basic Books, 1988.

Krumm, Rt. Rev. John R. *AIDS and God's Love.* Cincinnati: Forward Movement Publications, 1987.

Levy, Leonard. *The Establishment Clause: Religion and the First Amendment.* New York: Macmillan Publishing Co., 1986.

Lincoln, Abraham. *The Collected Works of Abraham Lincoln.* Edited by Roy Basler. New Brunswick, N.J.: Rutgers University Press, 1953.

Low Income Housing Information Service. *Federal Spending for Housing 1976–1990.* Washington, D.C.: Government Printing Office, 1989.

Lowell, James Russell. "Ode Recited at the Harvard Commemoration, July 21, 1865." In *The Complete Poetical Works of James Russell Lowell*, Cambridge Edition of the Poets, edited by Horace E. Scudder. Boston: Houghton Mifflin Co., 1897.

Maier, Pauline. *The Old Revolutionaries: Political Lives in the Age of Samuel Adams.* New York: Albert A. Knopf, 1980.

Malone, Dumas. *Jefferson and His Time.* Vol. 1, *Jefferson the Virginian.* Boston: Little, Brown & Co., 1948.

Massachusetts Council of Churches. *Abortion Amendment: Reproduction Question #1: No!* Boston: Massachusetts Council of Churches, 1986.

Mead, Sidney E. *The Lively Experiment.* New York: Harper & Row, 1963.

————. *The Nation with the Soul of a Church.* New York: Harper & Row, 1975. Reprint. Macon, Ga.: Mercer University Press, 1985.

Meek, Frederick M. "A Perspective on Twenty Years in Copley Square." A sermon preached at the Old South Church in Boston, October 30, 1966. Boston: Old South Church, 1966.

Morris, Richard B. *Witnesses at the Creation: Hamilton, Madison, Jay and the Constitution.* New York: Henry Holt, 1985. Reprint. New York: New American Library, A Plume Book, 1986.

Neuhaus, Richard. *The Naked Public Square.* Grand Rapids, Mich.: Wm. B. Eerdmans Publishing Co., 1984.

New York Times. 23 March 1981; 26 January, 3, 7 February 1984; 24, 31 October 1988.

Niebuhr, Reinhold. *The Children of Light and the Children of Darkness.* New York: Charles Scribner's Sons, 1944.

_____. "The Christian Witness in the Social and National Order." In *Christian Realism and Political Problems.* New York: Charles Scribner's Sons, 1953.

_____. "The Wise Men and the Mighty Men." In *Reflections on the End of an Era.* New York, London: Charles Scribner's Sons, 1936.

_____. "The Christian Witness in a Secular Age." In *Christianity and Power Politics.* New York: Charles Scribner's Sons, 1952.

_____. "Christian Faith and Political Controversy." In *Love and Justice: Selections from the Shorter Writings of Reinhold Niebuhr,* edited by D. B. Robertson. Philadelphia: Westminster Press, 1957.

_____. "Morality and Politics." In *Essays in Applied Christianity,* edited by D. B. Robertson. New York: Meridian Books, A Living Age Book, 1959.

_____. "The Religion of Abraham Lincoln." *Christian Century,* 10 February 1965: 173.

Novak, Michael. *Choosing Our King.* New York: Macmillan Publishing Co., 1974.

Office of the Secretary of State. "Government Aid to Non-Public Schools and Students." Boston: Office of the Secretary of State, Commonwealth of Massachusetts, 1988.

_____. *Massachusetts Information for Voters: The Ballot Questions in 1988.* Boston: Office of the Secretary of State, Commonwealth of Massachusetts, 1988.

_____. "Regulating or Prohibiting Abortion." Boston: Office of the Secretary of State, Commonwealth of Massachusetts, 1988.

Old South Church in Boston. *Annual Record.* Boston: The Old South Church in Boston, 1940–41.

_____. *Purpose and Bylaws.* Boston: The Old South Church in Boston, 1973.

Paton, Alan. *For You Departed.* New York: Charles Scribner's Sons, 1965.

Pilgrim Hymnal. New York: Pilgrim Press, 1958.

Quoist, Michel. "Lord, Why Did You Tell Me to Love?" In *Prayers.* Translated by Agnes M. Forsyth and Ann Marie de Commaille. Kansas City, Mo.: Sheed & Ward, 1963.

Reader's Digest Editors, eds. *Man of the Century: A Churchill Cavalcade.* Boston: Little, Brown & Co., 1965.

Robinson, Christine R. *Planning: AIDS.* Boston: United Way of Massachusetts Bay, 1987.

Ruether, Rosemary Radford. "Topics in Feminist Theology." In *Sexism and God-Talk: Toward a Feminist Theology.* Boston: Beacon Press, 1983

Schlesinger, Arthur M., Jr. *Robert Kennedy and His Times.* Boston: Houghton Mifflin Co., 1978.

Sherry, Paul H., ed. *The Riverside Preachers.* New York: Pilgrim Press, 1978.

Smart, James D. *The Quiet Revolution.* Philadelphia: Westminster Press, 1969.

Smith, George Adam. *The Book of the Twelve Prophets.* Rev. ed. Vol. 2. New York: Harper & Brothers, 1928.

Stackhouse, Max. *Public Theology and Political Economy.* Grand Rapids, Mich.: Wm. B. Eerdmans Publishing Co., for the Commission of Stewardship of the National Council of the Churches of Christ in the U.S.A., 1987.

Stein, Harry. *Ethics and Other Liabilities.* New York: St. Martin's Press, 1982.

Trueblood, Elton. *Abraham Lincoln: Theologian of Anguish.* New York: Harper & Row, 1973.

Tutu, Desmond. *Crying in the Wilderness*. Grand Rapids, Mich.: Wm. B. Eerdmans Publishing Co., 1982.

Village Voice. 29 December 1987.

Wallis, Jim. *Agenda for Biblical People*. New York: Harper & Row, 1976.

Weems, Ann. *Family Faith Stories*. Philadelphia: Westminster Press, 1985.

Weil, Simone. *Waiting for God*. New York: Harper & Brothers, Harper Colophon Books, 1951.

Winthrop, John. "A Model of Christian Charity." In *1493–1754: Discovering a New World*. Vol. 1 of *Annals of America*, edited by Mortimer Adler. Chicago: Encyclopaedia Britannica, 1976.